They Built the Earth

Then seeded life 3.7 billion years ago — it's
time to unlock the message they left

By Christopher Knight

and

Alan Butler

They Built the Earth

Then seeded life 3.7 billion years ago — it's
time to unlock the message they left

By Christopher Knight
and
Alan Butler

6TH
BOOKS

London, UK
Washington, DC, USA

CollectiveInk

First published by Sixth Books, 2025
Sixth Books is an imprint of Collective Ink Ltd.,
Unit 11, Shepperton House, 89 Shepperton Road, London, N1 3DF
office@collectiveinkbooks.com
www.collectiveinkbooks.com
www.6th-books.com

For distributor details and how to order please visit the 'Ordering' section on our website.

Text copyright: Christopher Knight and Alan Butler 2024

ISBN: 978 1 80341 964 0
978 1 80341 965 7 (ebook)
Library of Congress Control Number: 2024945775

A CIP catalogue record for this book is available from the British Library.

Design: Lapiz Digital Services

UK: Printed and bound by 4edge Limited
Printed in North America by CPI GPS partners

We operate a distinctive and ethical publishing philosophy in
all areas of our business, from our global network of authors to
production and worldwide distribution.

Contents

Preface

This small book has taken us a quarter of a century to research and write; not because the facts we present are at all complex, but rather the sheer scale and importance of what we have found has required us to consider a huge breadth of subjects. We did not set out to try and find the origins of life on Earth, let alone identify a clear and urgent message from the entity that created it. The hard facts unfolded to us by accident whilst we were involved in an entirely unrelated research project.

What we present here is unequivocal evidence that our planet and its moon were engineered as a highly sophisticated incubator, after which the Earth was seeded with DNA based bacteria of great complexity. This claim will seem incredible to many, who have been brought up to believe either in their religious scriptures or inaccurate science as explanations for the origin of our fertile world. We cannot debate with people who are driven by faith alone but we will surprise anyone who takes science seriously. On the way we quote many of the world's leading thinkers and present checkable facts to demonstrate that the existence of intelligent life on Earth is no happy accident.

Leading scientists today are well aware that much of what is taught in our schools and broadcast through our media is plain wrong. The Falsification Principle, originally proposed by Karl Popper, is today considered a fundamental hallmark of science. It states that any theory has to be capable of being tested and potentially proven to be false for it to be considered scientific. The idea that living entities arrived as a result of a lightning strike hitting water containing a mix of dumb chemical elements is known to be wrong, and the often repeated origin of the Moon being down to a Mars sized planet hitting the Earth has been shown to be impossible. Yet these sorts of notions are hard to shift from our cultural myths.

Science moves forward by a process of elimination and refinement of inspired ideas from the Big Bang to evolution. Occasionally when new evidence comes to light, even well-embedded theories have to be refined or possibly ejected. But nature abhors a vacuum and until replacement theories have percolated down from our finest brains, there is a great deal of reluctance to jettison outdated thinking.

We humans generally need a storyline to which we can subscribe, and that is why many people believe our lives are the gift of deities, whilst others subscribe to the 'happy accident of chemistry' notion. But hard-nosed, atheist scientists have in recent times expressed a view that life on Earth is no accident. The much respected British Astronomer Royal, Sir Fred Hoyle, is on record as saying:

Rather than accept that the fantastically small probability of life having arisen through the blind forces of nature, it seemed better to suppose that the origin of life was a deliberate intellectual act. By "better" I mean less likely to be wrong.

Shortly afterwards the eminent philosopher, Professor Antony Flew, who was renowned for his lifelong opposition to religious belief and defence of science, said in his eighties that in the face of new evidence he had had to change his mind. He stated:

A super-intelligence is the only good explanation for the origins of life and the complexity of nature.

Antony Flew was a leading figure in the analytic and evidentialist schools of thought who wrote extensively on the philosophy of religion. He was a strong advocate of atheism, arguing that one should presuppose atheism until evidence suggesting a God surfaces. This brave and monumental volte-face was entirely scientific. Flew did not believe that this super-intelligence was some kind of deity, and he certainly did not change his mind on the futility of ideas such as prayer or life after death.

What we have found, largely by accident, is a deliberate and detailed message from the entity that Flew called "a super-intelligence". Because it uses the language of mathematics it is readily falsifiable and therefore has to be described as scientific. The mathematics is very simple to follow and check, yet the unerring exactitude and repetition make this unmistakably a detailed message.

This message is not from some distant aliens or from a passing intergalactic spaceship but, we will demonstrate, from the intelligence so advanced that it engineered our planet and the Moon some 4.7 billion years ago, before seeding bacteria here. And this communication points very clearly at the greatest treasure of knowledge imaginable, that it has left for us to open and study.

We believe that this contact will transition humankind from its past infancy and its current adolescence into true species adulthood. We will be ready to grow into our new role of helping shape the universe. Please read the evidence we lay out here and make your voice heard in the demand that a team of top international experts are empowered to follow through on this — the most important project ever.

Chapter One

A New Dawn

When we published our book *Who Built the Moon?* in 2005 we were unsure what the reaction would be. At the time it seemed a distinct possibility that we would be attacked on all sides by astronomers and especially physicists for daring to point out that there is a whole range of evidence pointing to Earth's Moon being an engineered object, a deliberately created structure that had been put in place over four billion years ago in order to help make the Earth a haven for life. We were fully braced to defend our findings, and since our hypothesis was based primarily on math we had ensured that our work had been checked carefully by some of the best mathematicians we could find. Anyone might disagree with what we were suggesting but we knew for a fact that we could not be criticised for mathematical inaccuracy.

The sales of the book went ahead and reviews started to roll in. From the moment the book appeared we began to receive an average of four and a half stars on Amazon from those who had bought and read the book, a situation that has continued up to the present day. On the rare occasions when someone raised a negative point it was usually self-evident from their comments that they had either not read the book at all or had misunderstood what we had written. Overwhelmingly the vast majority of readers considered our stance to be sensible and well presented.

What we did not receive was even the tiniest comment from those whose job it was to know about the nature of the solar system. When we did get any reaction from professionals it tended to come from those who had retired and who were not at the time still tied to universities or institutes. Such reactions tended to be very constructive, and this caused us to

1

think about the overall situation. It did not take long for us to understand why our work was not criticised in any way by those at the leading edge of physics. What we were suggesting was very contentious and if accepted must instantly overturn the established and accepted explanation of the origins of the Earth and its Moon. The implications were colossal. Any expert who at the time was employed in academia would have been taking a massive gamble had he or she spoken out in defence of what we were suggesting. Even criticising our hypothesis, assuming they were inclined to do so, might be seen as 'engaging with the enemy' and so it was best for those who held chairs and who were comfortably ensconced and conscious of the need to preserve research grants to maintain an absolute silence on the subject.

Part of the remit of *Who Built the Moon?* was to list the many ways in which our planet was supported by the presence of such a large companion and to demonstrate what the Earth would have been like now if the Moon had not been present, or if it had been a much smaller body such as the moons of Mars for example. This was a subject that had hardly been mentioned previously, and judging by the reviews we received was a large part of the reason why the book was generally so well received.

All of this is not to suggest that our findings were ignored by people with influence, even if we did not get the credit for our observations. Almost as if a trigger had been pulled, astronomers suddenly began to make reference to the Moon and to its all-important role in nurturing life on Earth. This began within a short time after the publishing of the book, and made itself felt in the proliferation of television documentaries about the Moon and the bearing it had on the Earth that appeared at this time. The BBC website still contains educational videos that we are certain were written and produced as a direct result of *Who Built the Moon?* We know this because the production company consulted with us to create titles such as 'Why the Moon is still such a mystery' and 'Why water is one of the weirdest things in the universe'. We cannot help but wonder how many more documentaries were produced without reference but still as a direct result of reading our book.

One individual who was amazed at the content of our book was the famous movie director Roland Emmerich, who is well regarded for movies such as *Independence Day, White House Down,* and a raft of others. We became aware of this when we came across a discussion on the upcoming movie called *Moonfall* on a review website called screenrant.com, which referred to an interview with Emmerich where he credits our book *Who Built the Moon?* as his inspiration, saying:

The book written by Christopher Knight and Alan Butler explores the mysteries of the moon through geometry, astrophysics, and history. Emmerich says reading this book gave him the idea that the moon is "built rather than natural."

Prior to its release in early 2022 Emmerich gave a video interview regarding his new blockbuster movie, *Moonfall.* Here he states from the outset how the idea that the Moon was built had fascinated him and he decided to write and direct *Moonfall,* centred on the concept that the Moon was indeed an artificial object and that it had been placed in position by extraterrestrials to help make the Earth habitable.

So apparently captivated had Roland Emmerich been with our book that he had even written us, as the authors, into the script of his very expensive movie. The hero of the story, and the man who ultimately saves the Earth at the end of the movie, is a character who was referred to throughout the movie as KC Houseman. It was immediately obvious that the initials K and C are a reversal taken from Christopher Knight and the name Houseman is a direct synonym for the term 'Butler', from Alan Butler. To add to the reference to us, whilst everyone else in the movie is American, the hero of the story is British and speaks with a northern English accent; just as we both do. This of course made us smile and we took it as a sort of compliment from Roland Emmerich. To complete the reference to us he even chose an actor with a striking resemblance to Alan Butler.

Left is KC Houseman in Moonfall *and right Alan Butler in the same setting.*

Moonfall is a typical Hollywood science fiction romp that takes our core idea to weird and wonderful lengths in the name of entertainment — but for us the reality of the Moon is far more amazing than any amount of impossible, imagined events.

We suspect that a great deal more significant than *Moonfall* in terms of a response to our book was the Dawn Space Mission that was launched by NASA in September of 2007 and which, there is good reason to believe, was turned from a shelved mission back into a reality because of information we put forward in *Who Built the Moon?*

Humans have been observing the other objects in our solar system, and of course also the vastness of space far from our own back yard for quite some time. Beyond naked eye observation, which has been taking place for as long as human beings have lifted their gaze from the ground, the first magnifying telescopes began to appear after the start of the 17th century, though these were low in power and offered little in the way of evidence of anything much further away than the Moon. So inadequate were these first telescopes that one early sky watcher, the genius Galileo, using a low powered instrument was of the opinion that what we now know as ringed Saturn was a planet with 'handles'. Gradually the situation improved and by the time the first space probes left the Earth, humanity already knew a fair amount about the nature of some of our neighbours — and high powered telescopes, both optical and radio, were allowing us to look deep into the cosmos.

When local space flight became a possibility in the 1960s it was not long before scientists wanted to know more about the Moon and planets than could be assessed by way of even powerful Earth based telescopes, and within a short time the first probes were speeding through the blackness of space on epic journeys. The first long distance probe was named Voyager One and it commenced its incredible travels on September 5th, 1977. This remarkable craft made fly-bys of Jupiter, Saturn and Saturn's largest moon Titan. Voyager One is still travelling and is now passing out of the solar system altogether. Unless something gets in its way it will continue to travel indefinitely.

The view that the Voyager missions had of some of the moons of the gas giants made Earth scientists hungry to know more. Although the planets themselves are of tremendous interest, these days it is the moons of Jupiter, Saturn, Uranus, and Neptune that fascinate Earth based scientists the most. This is partly because these moons offer such a variety of different environments, and now that humanity is beginning to understand from some of the remoter and less hospitable parts of our own planet that life is incredibly adaptable, the search is on to see if it has managed to gain a foothold on some of the alien little worlds that are spinning around the gas giants, so far away from us. Sadly, in our opinion the results are likely to lead to disappointment.

The more humanity learns about these alien moons, the more it wishes to know, and so in addition to focusing on much nearer companions such as Venus or Mars, frequent missions are being sent much further — taking years to reach their targets and eventually sending back information that is often as puzzling as it is fascinating.

Jupiter has an estimated 79 moons! Many of these are extremely small but there are also bigger and particularly interesting examples, whilst the moon count for Saturn is now 150, and the number in both cases is growing all the time. Many of these moons have potential as places where life might have managed to gain a precarious hold and as a result scientists here on Earth would love to visit them all. Sadly, both time and cost prevent more than a very few deep space probes being sent to these far reaches of the solar system, and the list of destinations where physicists and astronomers would wish to send exploratory craft is always going to be far greater than practicality or economies can manage.

This being the case, it remains something of a mystery why, in the years running up to 2005, it was decided to send a space probe to the humble asteroid belt — specifically to look at the asteroids Vesta and Ceres. The asteroid belt is aptly named because it is simply a belt of rocky debris that maintains an orbit around the Sun between Mars and Jupiter. The Dawn craft was designed to look at the two largest members of the asteroid family. At first impression it seems strange that so many millions of dollars should be expended on achieving a better understanding of what are, in the case of Vesta, a large piece of uninspiring rock, and Ceres, a diminutive world, with only just enough mass to hold itself together as a sphere.

When quizzed as to the purpose of the Dawn mission, which by the time it was complete cost an estimated half a billion dollars, NASA stated that its purpose was to look at the boundaries of the rocky inner planets and the gas giants, and to allow us to better understand the origin and evolution of the solar system. How disappointed some of those at NASA must have been by the prospect of this particular mission when they were champing at the bit to know more about the moons of Jupiter, Saturn, Uranus, and Neptune — or even about the gas giants themselves. NASA stated that the name of the project, 'Dawn', had been chosen because the mission hoped to learn more about the dawn of the solar system. As a result of all we have learned since we began to look at the Dawn mission, we are not remotely convinced by either NASA's stated reasons for instigating the project or the explanation of its chosen name. Although the idea of such a mission was first mooted before *Who Built the Moon?* was published in 2005, it was put aside but then suddenly and unexpectedly revived. It seems entirely possible that our findings were a contributing factor in the decision to bring the Dawn mission out of mothballs rather quickly.

A great deal had already been ascertained about the asteroid belt long before Dawn was launched on September 27th, 2007. The asteroid belt certainly contains hundreds of thousands of rocks, perhaps many more than a million in total. Many of these are extremely small but some are sizeable. The biggest of the rocky asteroids in the belt is Vesta, which has an irregular shape described as an oblate spheroid, with a mean diameter of 525 kilometres. Vesta was first described in 1807 by the German astronomer Heinrich Willhelm Matthias Olbers who named it after the Roman goddess of hearth and home.

Even before the Dawn spacecraft arrived at Vesta in July of 2011, there was no real mystery surrounding this misshapen asteroid. Around two billion years ago and again about one billion years ago, Vesta was involved in a couple of collisions with other asteroid rocks that detached sizeable parts of it. Many of these displaced fragments were catapulted into space, and some of them found their way to the Earth, where we call them howardite, eucrite or diogenite meteorites. These fragments have proved to be an invaluable source of evidence regarding the nature and make-up of Vesta and the rocky members of the asteroid belt generally, which is probably not surprising when it is realised that there are at least 1200 pieces of Vesta on Earth and available for study.

The Dawn probe went into orbit around Vesta on July 16th, 2011, and although its reasons for being there might be considered as 'tenuous' there is no doubting the massive achievement of sending the ion driven spacecraft on such an epic journey and then being able to establish an orbit around an object that is 170 million kilometres away.

Vesta was studied in detail by the equipment aboard Dawn — a spacecraft not much bigger than a motorcycle, for just over a year, and then on September 5th, 2012, it departed Vesta and began its flight to the much more potentially interesting minor planet Ceres. The change of location went without a hitch and on March 6th, 2015, Dawn dropped into orbit around the first minor planet that had been examined close-up.

There can surely be no doubt that the time spent by Dawn at Vesta, though useful, was actually little more than a practice for what was to follow. Vesta did not turn out to be anything other than was expected, which, considering that large chunks of it had been studied for so long at first hand, was not entirely surprising. But the spherical planet Ceres was a different matter altogether. Even so, the most interesting aspect of Ceres lay in trying to understand why it exists at all and in particular the reason for it being in such a strange location.

By the standards of objects in the solar system Ceres is fairly diminutive in size, but it is still big enough to contain at least one quarter of all the mass to be found in the entire asteroid belt. Because of where it is, Ceres itself was originally often referred to as an asteroid but by almost any definition this is entirely the wrong name for this strange little world. Asteroids come in many different forms but in the main they tend to be rocky — usually solid rock. They may be formed from complex compounds, and when it comes to understanding how and when the solar system came into existence they are indeed interesting. Space is filled with all manner of debris, some of which are parts of asteroids that have been smashed in impacts with their companions and knocked off course. When these objects cross the path of the Earth, some of them are captured by Earth's gravity and are pulled to the ground, as was the case with the Vesta examples. At this point of entry to our atmosphere they are described as meteorites. The vast majority of this sort of debris burns up before it impacts the planet's surface, but some survive the heat generated by friction, and there are teams of people in various parts of the world whose entire careers are spent seeking out fallen meteorites that can be examined and classified.

Any one of the thousands of asteroids in the asteroid belt could one day be thrown off course, smashed to pieces and eventually end up as meteor showers that enliven our night skies but Ceres is different altogether than any asteroid, and orbiting where it does, it is so alien in comparison with its companions that it seems like the proverbial 'lonely little petunia in an onion patch'.

It appears that a large percentage of the interest NASA had in Ceres lay in trying to understand how something so different ended up where it is. The components of which it is made could not have come from the part of space in which it now orbits, if it is a considered a natural object. For this reason Ceres has often been thought of as an interloper; a rogue body that must have somehow become detached from its initial orbit — somewhere much further out in space, which then just happened to take up residence in the asteroid belt at some point in the distant past. This once seemed to be the only rational explanation for Ceres' presence, and in order to establish whether or not it was the case, it was important to discover exactly what kind of world Ceres is and to establish the elements from which it is made.

Even prior to the Dawn mission, Ceres had been extensively studied. It is possible, using the latest technology, to ascertain a great deal more about other worlds than one might expect in the case of such distant objects. To discover what they are made of, astronomers rely on what is known as spectroscopy. This works by spreading out the light given off or reflected from an object and then studying the wavelengths of that light. Every element with which we are familiar has its own, distinctive fingerprint in terms of light. Using a fairly complex process it is therefore possible to identify the components of even a very remote object. This process is possible, even with extremely distant stars, and although Ceres is a tiny object it is not massively distant in relative terms — so working out the chemicals that went into its make-up is fascinating but not incredible by modern standards. Of course it is always more advantageous to study any object in space at first hand, which is why spacecraft such as Dawn are so important, but it is unlikely that the experts at NASA discovered much about the composition, mass or orbit of Ceres that they did not already know.

Ceres most probably has a small, perhaps rocky core, but the vast majority of the little world is made up of water ice, clays, and chemicals such as ammonia. Ceres is very light in terms of its mass and this is due in the main to the fact that so much water has gone into its composition. It has been suggested that up to 200 million cubic kilometres of water could be held in Ceres' mantle, and if so, this would mean that as tiny as Ceres is, it has more water than the entire Earth!

Ceres does have some very unusual features such as its cryovolcanoes, which are volcanoes that throw out water vapour rather than super-hot magma that we see on rocky planets like our own. This process is often referred to as 'outgassing' and is something that is typical of comets. More elevated regions on the surface of Ceres may be due to previous episodes of cryovolcanic activity, and Ceres also sports a number of craters as a result of impacts — though probably not as many as had been expected. The reason for this is because of the nature of

Ceres' composition. Ceres seems to have the ability to quite quickly swallow objects that strike it — and to even eventually eradicate any crater that may have been formed by the impact.

One aspect of Ceres that Earth-bound scientists were keen to take a look at from a closer perspective than was possible from Earth was a series of very bright patches on the surface of the minor planet, that have appeared only very recently indeed. So bright are these new patches when the Sun is shining on Ceres that they had been observable through telescopes for some time prior to the Dawn mission. It was eventually announced that these very bright patches are related to the presence of 'salts' that have leeched out from the below the surface of Ceres. The patches most likely contain hydrated magnesium sulphate, and they could have some relationship with ammonia rich clays which form part of the surface of this intriguing little world.

The Dawn spacecraft arrived at Ceres on March 6th, 2015. It was put through a series of different manoeuvres in the months that followed, and its orbit was modified in order to achieve alternative objectives. By June of 2016 Dawn was still behaving well and offering useful information, and it was mooted that the craft might be sent on a further journey in order to take a look at another asteroid in the belt. This request was somewhat mysteriously refused by those in charge of the mission, and so Dawn began an extended stay in its orbit of Ceres. This continued until June 20th, 2017, at which time the mission officially came to an end. During this time Dawn orbited Ceres time and again, making Ceres one of the objects most 'studied' by any visiting spacecraft from the Earth. Exactly 'why' NASA chose to search the surface of Ceres so diligently and for so long might have seemed something of a mystery to most — but did not seem quite so puzzling to us. The spacecraft remained in orbit and also in contact with mission control until, reportedly, on October 31st, 2018, at which time it was suggested that it had run out of hydrazine propellant and as a result it supposedly lost contact with Earth. According to NASA, Dawn will continue to orbit Ceres for at least twenty years beyond 2018, until its orbit finally decays. In the meantime it has become, in the words of NASA, a "monument". If this is indeed a suitable name for what Dawn has become, it has the unique distinction in our estimation of being 'a monument upon a monument'.

The Dawn of a New Mindset at NASA

The Dawn Mission was considered a success for NASA — but that success was so pivotal it appears to have changed the Administration's entire weltanschauung regarding extraterrestrials. Previously they had been somewhat coy about discussing the possible existence of alien activity in our vicinity; yet just weeks before Dawn officially stopped transmitting, that changed. On 31st October 2018, NASA announced that it was, "Taking a new look at searching for life beyond Earth". It organised a workshop on the subject of 'Technosignatures' described as "any measurable property or effect that provides scientific evidence of past or present technology beyond Earth". Its stated aims included the question:

> What new surveys, new instruments, technology development, new data-mining algorithms, new theory and modelling, etc, would be important for future advances in the field?

Dear NASA, We can help you with a fully formed and evidenced theory for the biggest 'technosignature' imaginable.

Chapter Two

In the Beginning

It is easy to talk about huge numbers such as 'billions' but it is as good as impossible to really comprehend such enormous quantities. We humans tend to consider Earth to be 'our' planet, so is sobering to realise that our species, Homo sapiens, only arrived 300,000 years ago whilst life has existed on the Earth for around 3.7 billion years. To get some insight into what that means if we liken the timescale of all life on the Earth to a 24-hour day, we have only been around since a mere 7 seconds before midnight. This means that for 23 hours, 59 minutes, and 53 seconds there was no truly intelligent species inhabiting the Earth. By comparison dinosaurs did not exist until a hundred minutes ago and even flowers did not put in an appearance until well into the last hour.

A question that has occurred to many thinkers — and which any reader of this book might reasonably ask is: are there any grounds for supposing that life on our planet was a deliberate act rather than a happy accident that was followed by a process of evolution from the assumed 'primordial soup' through to humans today? The answer is an unequivocal yes, because whilst school textbooks continue to describe an entirely blind Darwinian mechanism that relies on an unbroken chain of accidental improvements, from the earliest single-celled creatures to invertebrates then to reptiles, onwards to mammals, to hominids and finally ourselves, serious scientists know that the true story is far less clear cut than was once thought. Yet many educated people, including some academics, hide from the hard truth and turn a blind eye to the subject; because to face up to the inevitable conclusion would be so disruptive to their established and comfortable world view.

When the Earth formed 4.54 billion years ago it was a ball of molten rock. As it slowly cooled, an atmosphere formed, mostly composed of gases spewed from the volcanoes that covered the young planet. It included hydrogen sulphide, methane, and as much as 200 times the amount of carbon dioxide as the current atmosphere. After about half a billion years, Earth's surface had solidified enough for water to collect on it. Despite the unbelievable hostility of the environment, it quickly became inhabited by a host of microorganisms, and life in one form or another soon existed in every nook and cranny — from mountain peaks to the bottom of the oceans. All other worlds in our solar system appear to be lifeless yet somehow Earth's barren rocks, sands, and assorted chemicals uniquely stirred and formed themselves into self-replicating life.

It was once thought that as life was unlikely to have appeared in a fully functional state, rather it must have started with just one of its necessary components in place and somehow or other attracted the other requisites to it; or else in some mysterious way it could have created the additional components that were required in order for it to function. Critics have pointed out that this would be like attempting to build a car by constructing a chassis and then simply hoping that wheels, an engine, and all the other necessary components would spontaneously appear. Yet the alternative — that life could have emerged of its own accord, fully formed and functional — did not stack up any better. Despite centuries of very detailed microbial research within the historical record, no trace of any life forms has been found that are simpler than bacteria: and bacteria themselves are far from simple. This is due to the fact that all bacteria contain the complete and elegant double-helix language that is deoxyribonucleic acid, generally known as DNA.

However, there is an insurmountable problem with the old — and often still trotted out idea — that a brew of chemicals in Earth's early atmosphere or on its surface suddenly transmogrified into bacteria.

Back in 1953 when the scientists James Watson and Francis Crick discovered the helical structure of the DNA molecule and then recognised the general way that it coded the formation and replication of proteins in cells, it seemed that a plausible scientific explanation for the origin of life was about to surface. The laboratory synthesis of amino acids from basic chemicals further heightened the expectation that we were on the verge of doing what we supposed the ancient Earth had mindlessly managed to achieve. We were about to create a living cell.

It was suggested that the early Earth, through a mixture of volcanic activity and landmass weathering, had acquired oceans rich in nutrients and chemicals — known as '*the primordial soup*'. It was in the constant intermixing of chemicals, and probably with the aid of lightning strikes, that the first primitive life must have come into existence — or so the evolutionists suggested. Experts remained confident that the primeval soup theory was the most likely explanation and were convinced that, given time, someone would manage to create life in a laboratory.

Soon after Watson and Crick's discovery, Stanley Miller, a graduate student from Chicago University, cooperated with Harold Urey, a Nobel Prize winner, to recreate the exact circumstances that are believed to have existed in the so-called primeval soup of the infant Earth. This soup contained water vapour, hydrogen, methane, and ammonia. Since it was estimated that lightning had played a part in the emergence of life, Miller and Urey provided an electrical spark to their chemical brew and eventually succeeded in creating simple amino acids. "Hooray," they and everyone else concerned said, because amino acids are a major component of organic life. Unfortunately, more than half a century later, no one has come any closer to actually creating life than this.

It has also been pointed out that the amino acids created by Miller, Urey, and others are only a tiny few of the constituents required for life. In any case the experiment was very selective in its methods. Amino acids are referred to as being left or right-handed, both of which were present in Miller and Urey's soup, whereas life itself uses only left-handed amino acids. What is more, the very electrical spark that created the amino acids would also have destroyed them, so they had to be artificially isolated in the experiment.

It might be thought reasonable that if life once formed in the oceans, it would continue to do so today. In reality this cannot happen because the mixture of temperatures, chemicals, and gases present is wrong. It was generally accepted that life could not have spontaneously appeared in an oxygen rich atmosphere and so the evolutionists had to suggest a very different sort of atmosphere on the infant Earth. (Oxygen, whilst preserving life, destroys organic molecules that are not alive.)

So, generating life in the laboratory proved to be utterly impossible, and researchers began to realise that new natural laws would need to be discovered to explain how the high degree of order and specificity of even a single cell could be generated by random, natural processes.

The DNA molecule occurs in the form of a double helix — rather like a ladder twisted into a spiral. The bases of the DNA are found in pairs, and these make up the rungs of the ladder that carry the information to replicate the entity in question.

When DNA copies itself, the ladder breaks down the middle of the rungs. New bases are matched to the bases of each upright and so the original DNA molecule then becomes two new identical molecules of DNA. Information necessary to build new proteins and to perform other necessary chemical changes is taken to various parts of a cell by another molecule, this one being ribonucleic acid (RNA). RNA is similar to DNA but is composed of only a single helix. RNA is therefore the 'messenger' that allows the information held within DNA to be distributed and acted upon.

An important question remains, and it is one that standard science still cannot answer. How did DNA come about in the first place, because as things stand now, only DNA can create DNA?

DNA is so incredibly complex that it is only now we are beginning to understand even a small part of how it truly functions or even what it is capable of doing. The truth is that for DNA to have assembled itself from the chemicals that were swilling about on the infant Earth would imply a level of improbability much greater than the number of known atoms in the entire universe! The inevitable conclusion is that it most certainly came into being somehow — but by simple chance? The mere suggestion that it could have done so should be considered ridiculous by anyone who had even the most rudimentary understanding of probability. The evidence suggests that IF every particle in the universe had one chance during each second since the beginning of time to become DNA — it still would not exist. As a result we are forced to the conclusion that there was, and perhaps still is, a mind of unimaginable power that stands behind life on Earth. But as we do not as yet know the identity of this entity, for the purpose of our own investigation we have assigned to it the title of Unknown Creative Agency (UCA).

As many leading authorities have already pointed out, it is futile to pretend that life on Earth somehow just happened one lucky day. An expert on the subject, Dr Robert Zubrin, put it rather well:

Believing that bacteria were the first life forms to emerge from chemistry is like believing that the iPhone was the first human-invented machine. This is incredible. Just as the development of the iPhone had to be preceded by the development of computers, radio, telephones, electricity, glassware, metallurgy, and written and spoken language, to name just a few necessary technological predecessors, so the creation of the first bacterium had to be preceded by the evolution of a raft of preceding biological technologies. But we see no evidence of any such history.

So the audit trail of life goes back to the tiny living creature that we call bacteria, which was and is, by any assessment, a massively complex self-replicating machine. And there it abruptly stops.

The Original Chicken and Egg Paradox

All life, as far as we know, is the result of the coding contained inside DNA. However, whilst all life is dependent on DNA, it is not necessarily a signature of living entities because genetic information in many viruses is also encoded in DNA, and viruses are not classified as truly alive since they are relatively simple and cannot exist without invading a living cell.

Viruses are commonly associated with causing disease and spreading pandemics such as the Covid-19 virus that hit the world hard so recently. Yet viruses are not always an enemy since they have also played an important role in human evolution — and without them none of us would exist.

Consider the Mabuya lizards that live in the Andes mountains of Colombia, which are very different to other reptiles that normally lay eggs with hard shells. This species actually gives birth to live young because the mothers have placentas: the specialised organs for feeding the developing young inside their bodies.

Placentas are more commonly associated with mammals like ourselves, but in 2001 zoologists Martha Patricia Ramírez-Pinilla and Adriana Jerez of the Industrial University of Santander in Bucaramanga, Colombia, described how Mabuya lizards also have extremely advanced placentas. Then in 2017

Ramírez-Pinilla got together with a team of geneticists led by Thierry Heidmann of Gustave Roussy in Paris and found that these lizards have a gene that is essential for the formation of the placenta, and that the gene in question came from a virus!

It seems that some 25 million years ago, the ancestors of these lizards were infected by a virus that incorporated some of its own DNA into their genome. But instead of being harmed, the lizards somehow meshed the viral DNA resulting in the development of placentas. It was entirely due to the presence of a virus that these reptiles evolved a highly complex new organ. We could not help but wonder whether the virus concerned was a throwback to the one that gave rise to the first mammals that appeared in the Triassic Period more than 200 million years ago as 'reprogrammed' members of the reptilian order Therapsida. It seems reasonable that the virus that caused the original switch from these Therapsida to mammals hung around and somehow repeated its trick with these South American lizards so relatively recently.

This suggests that such important evolutionary breakpoints are not a case of Darwinian trial and error, where some reptile DNA made a random mistake in replication that turned out to be beneficial, but a directional change caused by a third-party recoding by a non-living, yet DNA based 'machine'. Had the virus not performed in the way it did back in the Triassic Period there would have been no mammals, no hominids, and therefore no humans.

This would appear to be a good example of how standard Darwinian evolution is, at best, a very inadequate theory.

It has also recently been found by researchers at the Stanford University School of Medicine that genetic material from ancient viral infections was critical to human development in other ways. These researchers identified several noncoding RNA molecules of viral origins that are necessary for a fertilised human egg to acquire the ability in early development to become all the cells and tissues of the body. Blocking the production of this RNA molecule stops development in its tracks.

The discovery comes on the heels of an earlier Stanford study that showed that human embryos are packed full of what appear to be viral particles arising from similar left-behind genetic material. Vittorio Sebastiano, an assistant professor of obstetrics and gynaecology at Stanford, said:

> *"We're starting to accumulate evidence that these viral sequences, which originally may have threatened the survival of our species, were co-opted by our genomes for their own benefit."* He continued, *"In this manner, they may even have contributed species-specific characteristics and fundamental cell processes, even in humans."*[1]

He went on to point out how the virus mechanism appears to be an essential part of our existence:

> *This is the first time that these virally derived RNA molecules have been shown to be directly involved with and necessary for vital steps of human development ... What's really interesting is that these sequences are found only in primates, raising the possibility that their function may have contributed to unique characteristics that distinguish humans from other animals.*

So, whilst 'life' describes all kinds of organisms from cyanobacteria to plants and animals, it seems that we would not be here without the contribution of viruses. Again, it seems that evolutionary development is not just a happy internal accident of a DNA misprint. Rather it is a complex series of changes triggered by the timely arrival of a virus carrying a set of complementary instructions.

The essence of life is reproduction, the formation of identical or near identical copies of a complex structure from simple starting materials, critically adjusted from time to time by the presence of viruses. The ongoing increase of complexity involved in the formation of living organisms from their precursors distinguishes the processes of biological growth and reproduction, and sets them apart from physical processes such as crystallisation. This local increase of complexity can also be described as a decrease of entropy, which we have already speculated might be the motivation of the Unknown Creative Agency that seeded and promoted life on Earth.

All living organisms possess a genome, which is the set of instructions for making the body, and this is always composed of nucleic acid. It is usually DNA (deoxyribonucleic acid) or in the case of some viruses, RNA (ribonucleic acid). The genome consists of a number of genes each of which is a segment of nucleic acid coding for a particular type of protein molecule. In October 2004, French researchers announced findings that blurred the boundary once again. Didier Raoult and his colleagues at the University of the Mediterranean in Marseille announced that they had sequenced the genome of the largest known virus, Mimivirus, which had been discovered back in 1992. This virus, about the size of small bacterium, contained numerous genes previously thought to only exist in cellular organisms. The virus is therefore either a very smart bit of 'dead' matter or it is part of a unique club of entities only known to exist upon Earth. The unbelievable nature of living matter caused astrobiologist Paul Davies to observe in December 2004:

Most people take the existence of life for granted, but to a physicist like me it seems astounding. How do stupid atoms do such clever things? Physicists normally think of matter in terms of inert, clod-like particles jostling each other, so the elaborate organisation of the living cell appears little short of miraculous. Evidently, living organisms represent a state of matter in a class apart from the rest.

Some chromosomes contain extremely long strings of DNA of more than a metre in length, which is colossal considering the microscopic nature of the DNA molecule itself. However, the question that has puzzled everyone concerned is the origin of this process, because all enzymes are proteins and protein synthesis must be directed by DNA. However, DNA replication cannot take place without these proteins. So, what came first — the protein or the DNA?

Never mind the 'chicken and egg' conundrum; the problem goes right back to the origin of all life.

It is a problem that appears to have no answer. What is certain is that amino acids, nucleotides, lipids and other multi-atom molecules can be manufactured at random by heat, for example from lightning strikes. They can also come about from sunlight and other sources of energy that do not themselves have life. Many ideas have been put forward to explain the occurrence of DNA but at the end of the day none of them can be more than educated guesses. But as we were researching this book a new theory appeared and it is one that has gained favour with many experts. This theory suggests that DNA exists thanks to the presence of Earth's Moon!

Four billion years ago the orbit of the Moon was much closer to the Earth than it is today. At this time the Earth was spinning much faster on its axis and phenomenal tides were being raised on the Earth by the constant passing of the Moon. With the Moon so much closer to Earth at this time the height of the tides would have been colossal.

Richard Lathe, a molecular biologist at Pieta Research in Edinburgh, has suggested that within the primordial oceans, constantly dragged back and forth by the passing of the Moon, DNA could have been rapidly multiplied.[2]

One of the most commonly held theories regarding the origin of DNA is that it emerged when smaller, precursor molecules in the waters of the early oceans, the 'primordial soup', came together or were 'polymerised' into long strands. These long strands, it is suggested, became the templates for more molecules to attach themselves along the templates, which eventually resulted in double-stranded molecules like DNA.

Richard Lathe suggests that the problem lies in the need for some mechanism that would constantly break apart the double strands in order to keep the process going. He maintains it would have taken some external force to dissociate the two strands.

It is at around 50°C that single DNA strands act as templates for synthesising complementary strands, whereas at the higher temperature of about 100°C these double strands break apart and this doubles the number of molecules. When the temperature falls, the process begins again. The number of replications grows exponentially with just 40 cycles producing a trillion identical copies.

A billion years after the Moon came to orbit the Earth, it was still extremely close to its host planet, and because the Earth was spinning much faster than it is now, the Moon passed overhead much more often. Not only were the resultant tides more frequent, they were also much greater in force, and as Lathe suggests must have extended several hundred kilometres inland. This meant that coastal areas were subjected to rapid changes in salinity, and Richard Lathe suggests that this would have led to repeated and very frequent association and dissociation of double-stranded molecules similar to those of DNA.

As the huge tides advanced, salt concentrations would have been very low. Even modern double-stranded DNA breaks apart under such conditions because electrically charged phosphate groups on each strand repel each other. However, when the tides receded, precursor molecules and precipitated salt would have been present in high concentrations. Lathe claims that this would have encouraged DNA-like double-stranded molecules to form because high salt concentrations neutralise DNA's phosphate charges and this allows strands to stick together.

These constant salty cycles and changes in temperature are what Lathe suggests would have amplified molecules such as DNA but he points out that the tidal forces were absolutely vital in the process. Whilst it is true that the Sun also creates tides on the Earth, these are of a very low magnitude compared to those caused by the Moon, which although only a fraction of the size of the Sun is very much closer to Earth. Three billion years ago it was closer still.

We repeat that without DNA there could be no life because it stands at the very heart of the replication of living matter. From the single-celled amoeba to the largest blue whale on our planet, DNA is the vital component that began life and which keeps it going. Perhaps Richard Lathe is correct and it was the presence of so large a Moon that began the chemical process that led to us but it does remain a fact that despite all the theories, no scientist has yet managed to take the various chemicals that comprise life and arrange them in such a way that they become even the very simplest life form.

Lathe's theory could explain how the Moon caused the early replication of DNA but its origin remains a complete mystery, and many scientists are quite unsettled about the theory of how life came into existence in the first place. For example, Dr David A. Kaufmann of the University of Florida said:

> *Evolution lacks a scientifically acceptable explanation of the source of the precisely planned codes within cells without which there can be no specific proteins and hence, no life.*

Admittedly David Kaufmann is a creationist, so some people could be suspicious of his motivation for this conclusion. But then there is Professor Hubert P. Yockey, a physicist from the

University of California — who was most definitely not an adherent of religious creationism yet he was concerned that discredited ideas continue to clog up the process of seeking out the truth. He wrote:

> *Although at the beginning the paradigm was worth consideration, now the entire effort in the primeval soup paradigm is self-deception on the ideology of its champions...*
>
> *The history of science shows that a paradigm, once it has achieved the status of acceptance (and is incorporated in textbooks) and regardless of its failures, is declared invalid only when a new paradigm is available to replace it. Nevertheless, in order to make progress in science, it is necessary to clear the decks, so to speak, of failed paradigms. This must be done even if this leaves the decks entirely clear and no paradigms survive. It is a characteristic of the true believer in religion, philosophy and ideology that he must have a set of beliefs, come what may (Hoffer, 1951). Belief in a primeval soup on the grounds that no other paradigm is available is an example of the logical fallacy of the false alternative. In science it is a virtue to acknowledge ignorance. This has been universally the case in the history of science as Kuhn (1970) has discussed in detail. There is no reason that this should be different in the research on the origin of life.*

Yockey makes this statement because like many other scientists he cannot believe that the question regarding the emergence of life can be answered at all well by the invention of a notion such as a 'primordial soup'. It appears to be simply wrong and is obfuscating progress towards a plausible explanation.

The main reasons there is so much unrest about this question is because DNA cannot exist without life and life cannot exist without DNA. It occurs to us that even the theories of Richard Lathe on the way the Moon may have contributed to the rapid spreading of life through huge tides and chemical mixing comes no closer to explaining how life actually came about.

Some experts still claim that it must have all happened by accident, presumably because the other possibilities are too hard to swallow.

End Notes

1. https://med.stanford.edu/news/all-news/2015/11/ancient-viral-molecules-essential-for-human-development. html#:~:text="We%27re%20starting%20to%20accumulate, professor%20of%20obstetrics%20and%20gynecology

2. Lathe, R. "Fast Tidal Cycling and the Origin of Life". *The Journal Icarus* 168(1) (2004), pp. 18–22.

Chapter Three

The Probability Problem

Nobody doubts that the information contained in a single gene must be at least as great as the enzyme it controls. However, just one average protein contains over 300 amino acids. In order to create the protein it would take a gene of DNA that would have to contain 1000 nucleotides in its chain. Every DNA chain contains four sorts of nucleotides. This seems complicated but it results in a possible $4^{\times 10\ 1000}$ possible forms. For those who do not realise, $4^{\times 10\ 1000}$ represents the number 4 followed by 1000 zeros.

These are values beyond all comprehension. To get some perspective on this it interesting to note that it is estimated that there are only $10^{\times 10\ 80}$ particles in the whole universe. One begins to realise how utterly impossible it would have been for complex DNA to be accidentally created in the primeval soup of the young Earth.

In the world of probability some things are very likely to happen, others might sometimes happen, but some can never happen at all. An expert in probability, Émile Borel (1871–1956) claimed that phenomena with very small probability don't occur. He estimated that there would be about one chance in $10^{\times 10\ 50}$ for a small probability. Tiny though these odds were, they were not remote enough for more modern experts in probability. William M. Dembski, Associate Research Professor in the conceptual foundations of science at Baylor University and a senior fellow with Discovery Institute's Center for Science and Culture in Seattle, decided to go further. He estimated that there were $10^{\times 10\ 80}$ particles in the universe and wondered how many times per second an event might occur. The number he came up with was $10^{\times 10\ 45}$. He then calculated the number of seconds from the beginning of the universe to the present time, and then to make sure he was erring on the side of caution he multiplied this number by one billion and arrived at the number 10×10^{25} seconds. He now multiplied all the figures together achieving a result of 10×10^{150} for his Law of Small Probability.

For a minimum living cell there are 60,000 proteins of 150 configurations. Joseph A. Mastropaolo, PhD Kinesiology/ Physiology, an expert who has tackled this problem at length, estimates that the probability of the evolution of this first cell would be an absolutely staggering 1 in $10 \times 10^{4,478,296}$ or 10 followed by 4,478,296 zeros. This exceeds Dembski's estimation for Small Probability by such a great margin that were it not for the fact that DNA does clearly exist, no self-respecting scientist could uphold the possibility of it having originated by chance.

If every particle in the universe had one chance for every second since the beginning of time — we still would not have DNA.

In case there are readers who doubt Mastropaolo's scepticism regarding the possibility of DNA creating itself from scratch, it is interesting to see that he is far from alone. Peter T. Mora of Macromolecular Biology Section, Immunology Program, National Cancer Institute, Bethesda, Maryland, wrote:

The presence of a living unit is exactly opposite to what we would expect on the basis of pure statistical and probability considerations.

The English scientist JD Bernal said, way back in 1965:

The answer would seem to me combined with the knowledge that life is actually there, to lead to the conclusion that some sequences other than chance occurrences must have led to the appearance of life as we know it.

And to add to the list of dissenters regarding a theory that clearly doesn't hold water, primeval or not, we quote again the late Professor Sir Fred Hoyle, one of the most respected astronomers who has ever lived.

Rather than accept that fantastically small probability of life having arisen through the blind forces of nature, it seemed better to suppose that the origin of life was a deliberate intellectual act. By "better" I mean less likely to be wrong.

However, no matter how great and how many the howls of indignation at this complete disregard of probability, one of the fundamental tools of science, it remains a fact that DNA did occur somehow. As the saying goes, nature abhors a vacuum of any sort. No matter how much Professor Yockey may suggest that if we have no viable theory we should manage without it until one is discovered, it seems that to many scientists a twisted and broken paradigm is better than none at all.

After all, the alternative might be unthinkable to most experts. We may, for example, have to consider the possibility of a 'mind' behind the creation of DNA, even if we can accept evolution as a viable way forward once DNA existed. The majority of scientists would prefer to break their own rules rather than to evoke some variety of deity but even Professor Sir Fred Hoyle was left with the only conclusion that could occur to him, namely that the universe was under some sort of 'intelligent cosmic control'. Is this the way forward? If we are going to be truly honest, bearing in mind the utter impossibility of the chance occurrence of DNA, might we have to accept that 'God spoke and it was so'?

Who can blame Antony Flew for turning a lifetime's work on its head and saying:

A super-intelligence is the only good explanation for the origin of life and the complexity of nature

However, Flew's definition of a super-intelligence bears little resemblance to the deity of Judeo-Christian-Islamic tradition, which he describes as being depicted as "omnipotent Oriental despots — cosmic Saddam Husseins". He is actually describing something as open as our own 'Unknown Creative Agency' — which presumably might mean virtually anything from a sublime single entity to a galactic federation of life spreaders!

Given that it could not have sprung up fully formed through any amount of serendipity and that it would have been incapable of miraculously assembling all of its complex components, we have to conclude that the first bacteria came from somewhere else. This is a concept called panspermia. The notion goes back as far as the Ancient Greeks and in the modern era was further developed by leading experts such as Carl Sagan and Iosif Shklovskii and later by Francis Crick and Leslie Orgel. These commentators proposed that life on Earth was the result of a deliberate infection, designed and implemented by aliens. Interestingly it was the same Francis Crick who co-discovered the structure of DNA with James Watson back in the early 1950s.

Carl Sagan and Iosif Shklovskii coauthored a book with the title *Intelligent Life in the Universe* in 1966, in which they reviewed the evidence and proposed that life on the Earth is likely to have been seeded deliberately by an alien civilization. This was a concept they referred to as 'Directed Panspermia'.

It is now known that the age of the universe is 13.7 billion years, give or take 200 million years. If this is taken as being accurate it means that the universe has existed three times as long as the period of life on Earth, so there was plenty of time for a super-advanced species to develop and become so smart that it could take on the task of seeding planets with life. However, the latest estimation of the age of the universe, provided by the James Webb Telescope, is 27 billion years, leaving more than enough time for such a species to have appeared and even disappeared on a number of occasions.

Having pointed out that DNA, such as we see here on Earth, cannot have come into existence anywhere in the entire universe without assistance, the origin of the UCA itself must have been something very different. A Boltzmann brain (a super-intellect that instantly pops up fully formed from a void) perhaps, or an evolution from a chemistry that did have the requisite stages prior to bacteria forming, that are absent on Earth.

A Shotgun or a Sniper Rifle Approach

If this idea of 'directed panspermia' is real, it must have been conducted by a super-advanced entity or civilization, as the outstanding philosopher we previously quoted Antony Flew called it. It seems unlikely that these entities would have simply sprayed bacteria across star systems in galaxy after galaxy. That would be like a medieval farmhand throwing plant seeds around willy-nilly, regardless of the terrain or climate. A carefully targeted approach seems much more likely for aliens who must have been far in advance of our current level of development.

Modern precision farming techniques control every aspect of planting from carefully selecting the properties of the seed, preparing the soil chemistry, accurate spreading, heating, watering, and ensuring protection from external threats. Similarly, a super-intelligent species would apply a very discerning level of husbandry and prepare any potential host planet so as to ensure that the seeds of life it propagated had every chance of germinating and flourishing into useful specimens.

The idea that there are other forms of advanced life elsewhere in the cosmos does seem possible, even probable. In the winter of 1967 Cambridge radio astronomers discovered a new type of radio source from deep space of such an artificial seeming nature that it caused much excitement in the scientific community. They thought that they might have discovered an extraterrestrial intelligence that was reaching out across intergalactic space. The regular lighthouse-like rhythm appeared to be a cosmic beacon, but we now know that what they had discovered was pulsars; naturally occurring objects rather than anything artificial.

Partly at least as a result of the pulsar incident, looking out for incoming communications turned into a major industry and a classic example of 'shotgun' thinking can be found with the world's leading ET hunters — SETI (the Search for Extraterrestrial Intelligence). This much vaunted organization was founded on the principle that a hypothetical civilization on a far-flung world might seek to make their existence known by means of radio or light wave transmissions.

SETI has been diligently sweeping the heavens for decades but in 2016 a new $100 million project with a ten-year life began, based at Berkeley SETI Research Center at the University of California, Berkeley. Called 'Breakthrough Listen' the project was set up in the hope that it would discover signs of extraterrestrial civilizations by scanning selected stars and galaxies for radio signals and laser transmissions using radio telescopes that can cover ten times more sky than any previous searches. It began scanning the entire range of frequencies between 1 GHz and 10 GHz, which is considered to be the 'quiet zone' in the spectrum where radio waves are less obscured by cosmic sources or Earth's atmosphere. Described as the most comprehensive search for alien communications to date it is estimated that the project generates as much data in a single day as previous SETI projects could manage in a year.

SETI is looking towards all 43 neighbouring stars within a 16.3 light year range, and peeping at a thousand other stars and hundreds of galaxies that are many millions of light years away. Any message received from one of these particularly far-flung galaxies would therefore have been transmitted at least as far back as the time when early ape-like hominids such as Australopithecus afarensis (famous for the fossil we call 'Lucy') walked the plains of Africa. As a result, sending a reply would be pointless because our species would be long gone; perhaps evolved into something wonderful — or long-since destroyed before it reached its destination.

What exactly SETI hopes to find is unclear, but it must be something, anything that stands out from random background events to indicate intelligence — hopefully in the form of a message addressed to a relatively young life form like us, on the surface of a rocky planet circling a medium sized star that is just one of hundreds of billions in our galaxy alone.

Given the hundreds, thousands, or even millions of light years involved between transmission and reception the core idea of SETI has been likened to standing next to a public phone on a desert island, waiting for it to ring.

We somehow doubt it will.

Instead of spending so much money and time, and tying up prime scientific equipment on a mega long shot, we prefer the suggestion made by two leading physicists, Christopher Rose and Gregory Wright, when they said:

Rather than transmitting radio messages, extraterrestrial civilisations would find it far more efficient to send us a 'message in a bottle', some kind of physical message inscribed on matter. And it could be waiting for us in our own backyard.

This turned out to be true and, as we were to discover, in the case of Earth the message is itself the medium — rather than a mere carrier mechanism. If our infant planet was selected for seeding with DNA based life all that time ago, surely the rough and ready rocky sphere then present would have had to be turned into a haven for emerging life first: a gigantic incubator with a 4.5 billion year plan, leading to the point where the seeded bacteria would evolve into beings capable of space flight. These beings (us) are now ready and able to receive a contact message from our progenitors, followed by all the information we could possibly imagine.

This was a massively complex mission as the requirements for nurturing life are extremely complicated and many.

Taking Stock

The evidence, accepted by many very heavy-weight scientific thinkers, is that life on Earth cannot be due to random chemical happenstance and is likely to have resulted from 'directed panspermia'. This means that an intelligence we have called the Unknown Creative Agency (UCA) deliberately directed DNA based material at our planet shortly after the Earth/Moon duopoly came into existence.

At this stage it is worth reflecting on a key question this possibility raises.

We humans like to think we are not alone, either in terms of the fiction we create or in real-world scientific investment. Many hundreds of millions of dollars have gone into programs run by organizations such as SETI — which, as far as we know, has produced zero results. It is therefore reasonable to pose a question regarding the idea of alien contact. There are three main possible answers. The question is:

If a message from aliens was received would it most likely be:

a. A blind intergalactic ongoing broadcast like a mass-market leaflet that just happened to drop into our mailbox?

b. A targeted mail-shot aimed at planets with a defined profile type over hundreds of millions of years?

c. A precise correspondence addressed to the occupants of planet Earth timed for right now?

The whole idea of SETI appears to be based on the assumption that the answer is a). As far as we are aware there has been little, if any thought given to the far more likely answer of c).

A subordinate question that then raises its head is: In each of the above cases, what would be the motivation for initiating a contact message? A reasonable assumption would be for each:

a. Just saying "Hi" so you know you are not alone.
b. To provide some useful generic information.
c. To provide very specific information for the next stage of advanced life on Earth.

The following chapters will put forward more detailed evidence about how massively unlikely it is that we humans exist at all — unless we were planned. Then we will turn to the details of the first contact message and follow on with what we need to do next.

Chapter Four

An Incredible Double Act

The Earth teems with life. Across every square centimetre of its land masses, in lakes, rivers, and every ocean plants and creatures of one sort or another abound. This is particularly remarkable when one bears in mind that humanity has now sent spacecraft to many of the other planets and moons in our solar system without having yet encountered anything that even approximates life. On our own planet life appears to be irrepressible and manages to gain a foothold in places that once upon a time would have been considered far too extreme for anything to survive, and yet even deep on the ocean bed, around poisonous, super-hot volcanic smokestacks, where pressures are beyond fantastic, myriad living creatures are found that are self-evidently not simply somehow hanging on but positively flourishing.

It is clear that our planet is hugely unusual, and possibly unique. The Earth has an atmosphere rich in the very gases upon which life has come to rely. In addition, developing life has at its disposal the necessary minerals and metals that form the composition of all plants and creatures. Life exists amidst temperatures and pressures to which it has become adapted, and in conditions that allow it to proliferate across periods of settled time that simply would not occur elsewhere.

As a fairly small, rocky planet the Earth is not unusual, even in our own solar system. Mercury, Venus, Mars, and even Earth's Moon are in many respects similar to the Earth but in terms of what has happened to them across the last four billion years and more, each of them is dramatically different to our own world. Scientists search frantically to discover whether even the most primitive representative of life has somehow managed to evolve and grow on the Earth's sister planets, but up to the present time at least, investigators have been disappointed. Unless that picture changes and some form of simple life is found, perhaps on some of the more remote moons of the giant gas planets much further out in our solar system, it looks as though we are alone — the single representative of a living world in the entire solar system and just possibly anywhere.

At the time we began the research for our book *Who Built the Moon?* now well over two decades ago, astronomers and physicists had already begun to realise that in many respects the Earth had come to exist in a part of space that would prove to be very fortunate in comparison with the other terrestrial type planets. The Earth orbits at a distance from the Sun that is classed as being in the habitable zone. This is a region at which the Earth receives significant heat and light from our star, but not too much. For obvious reasons, often also referred to as the 'Goldilocks Zone', the distance of the Earth's orbit from the Sun allows water to exist in all its three forms, ice, liquid, and gas — which requires a very tiny span of temperatures — so small in fact that water is only liquid for less than one 10,000th of the range of temperatures found in our solar system!

However, this happy location could not be anything like enough to allow life to develop here because, like all the other planets, the Earth would soon fall prey to the deeply destructive outpourings of the Sun, were it not for one factor.

It happens that the composition of the Earth is of a very particular type. The molten core of our planet is rich in iron and nickel, which is constantly swirled around by the turning of the Earth and this provides the mechanism by which the Earth manages to stave off the worst excesses of the environment in which it exists. The Sun at the heart of our solar system is highly reactive and constantly hurls radiation of many different kinds into space, and it is within this highly poisonous environment that the Earth orbits. However, because of its iron and nickel rich core, the Earth is actually a massive natural dynamo, and dynamos create around themselves magnetic fields, of which the Earth's version is more significant than that of any of its sister planets. This magnetic field, better known as the magnetosphere, stands around the Earth and deflects a high percentage of the radiation sent out on the solar wind that would otherwise fall upon the surface of the planet, where it would immediately kill any form of life that managed to gain a toehold. The radiation is deflected harmlessly into space, creating an environment upon the surface of the Earth that is friendly to the forms of life that are to be found upon it.

In a significant number of respects, the Earth was a good candidate to become a haven for life but we should not be misled because there were also many other factors regarding the Earth to suggest that any life that might possibly develop here would be doomed to almost immediate extinction. Part of the problem was that some of what made the Earth potentially friendly to life, would also have been the cause of its demise.

At the start of the solar system, when the planets began to form at different distances from the Sun, and the Earth gradually coalesced into a ball, the heavier elements of its composition sank towards the centre and lighter rock remained on the surface. In its earliest days the planet's equator remained pointing directly at the Sun. This would have meant that the polar regions would have received virtually no light and heat, whilst the equatorial belt would have become hotter and hotter, providing no temperate zones or areas where water could exist in its liquid state. So despite the benefits of its perfect position relative to the Sun, the Earth was destined to end up as a planet with a thick, rocky crust similar to that of Mars. All the planet's minerals and metals would have remained locked into its core, and with an atmosphere of noxious gases and surface temperatures vacillating between catastrophically hot and indescribably cold, the prognosis would not have been good for any kind of life — let alone intelligent life.

Fortunately for us, something happened that changed the Earth's potential totally. Somehow, and we will go into this later, the Earth came into possession of an extremely large Moon. So big in fact is our Moon that the Earth and Moon together are sometimes described as being a double planet. Although in a strict sense this is not quite true, the Earth is only 3.66 times larger than the Moon in terms of size and this ensures that our Moon has a tremendous bearing on the way the Earth works. It is true that in its early days the relationship between the Earth and the Moon was a very violent one, but in the fullness of time it would be the very presence of the Moon that would allow the Earth to become a veritable incubator for life.

The Moon's critical importance was not spoken about much until around the time we published *Who Built the Moon?* in 2005 and it almost seems as though what we had to say in the book caused otherwise reticent astronomers and physicists to look at the Moon in a different way — or perhaps to come clean regarding what they had 'already' observed. It is true that a number of experts had previously expressed their amazement about an 'impossible' Moon, but the mainstream authorities were not yet ready to publicly discuss the possibility that the Moon just might be an artificial object, created specifically to promote a life-bearing Earth.

Impossible Numbers

We had come across a very strange aspect of the Earth/Moon relationship whilst researching a totally unconnected subject in the field of prehistoric systems of metrology, particularly regarding the unit that is known as the Megalithic Yard. The Megalithic Yard was part of an incredibly comprehensive geodetic system of measurements that was based on a precise awareness of the size of the sphere of Earth. Incredibly but irrefutably this system of measurement was clearly understood by some cultures at least four thousand years ago and possibly much longer. Whilst it may seem strange that people from the Stone Age had such scientific precision, our evidence has since been thoroughly checked by experts using reconstructions, and found to be correct. (See Chapter 11.)

What followed in our research astonishes us today just as much as it did over twenty years ago, but we stress that there is nothing conjectural about what we found — it is all provable fact. We went on to realise that the Moon also conformed precisely with this incredible mathematical and geodetic system, yet no other planet and its moon that we checked throughout the solar system enjoyed this kind of correlation. The super-ancient system of measurement we had discovered, and which we proved conclusively had existed, worked on an alternative form of geometry to the one we use today. It had 366 degrees in circles, rather than the 360 degrees we presently use, and as incredible as it seemed, there was no doubt that this form of geometry had been devised well over 4000 years ago. The reason that 366 degrees had been chosen was because the Earth revolves on its axis this number of times in one of its orbits around the Sun. (From an Earth based perspective we perceive 365 days in a year but that is because exactly one revolution on every orbit is lost due to the passage of the planet in that orbit.)

Meanwhile the Earth polar circumference divided into 366 equal parts (Megalithic degrees) produces a linear length that is equal to 100th of the lunar circumference — suggesting that while the Earth was originally split into 366 degrees, there are exactly 100 of the same degrees to the circumference of the Moon — a figure that is incredibly accurate.

But matters got even stranger the closer we looked.

The Sun has to be taken into account because, unlike its association with all the other major planets and moons of the solar system, it maintains a very strange integer relationship with both the Earth and our Moon. Seen from the surface of our planet, the Sun and the Moon appear to be the same size, which is why total solar eclipses happen. This is when the disc of the Moon precisely and seemingly miraculously perfectly obscures the Sun. Such a happening takes place because the Moon is 400 times smaller than the Sun but at the time of total solar eclipses it is also a neat 400 times closer to the viewer, making both the Sun and the Moon occupy about one half of a degree of the sky.

The Sun and the Moon appearing to be the same size when viewed from the Earth has been described as a most amazing coincidence by astrophysicists — but that fact would be absolutely stunning even if the repeating relations of circumference and distance were both some random number. But the fact that they are a very neat 400 in both respects seems odd to say the least.

At the time of writing *Who Built the Moon?* we came to the conclusion that these, and many other repeating integer values, were a sort of primordial signature left by some super-intellect that had engineered the Earth and constructed the Moon so that they demonstrated a cohesion with the physical reality of the Sun. It felt as if this was a 'signpost' intended for intelligent life forms on Earth; so was our attention being deliberately directed towards the nature of the Moon. Was the Earth's companion indeed artificial? And to what in particular is this potential 'signpost' pointing us?

We mused that there must be a message involved in what amounted to a wake-up call for humanity — but we just did not know where to look for the final piece of the jigsaw at that time. That was to present itself later.

The extreme oddity of the Moon had in fact been noticed long before our discoveries, and there were quite a number of heavy-duty scientists who had spotted the total improbability of our companion in space, but one had to search hard to find any published trace of their observations with this regard. From our own point of view, besides identifying the raft of physical 'coincidences' we also stressed how life on Earth owed everything to the size, mass, position, and complex movement of the Moon. Up to that time, the great disc in our night skies was largely taken for granted, but then something changed.

A Machine-like Efficiency

Not too long after publication, beautifully made television documentaries began to appear, which itemised the same observations we had made regarding everything the Moon had done and continues to do to safeguard our planet; to keep it upright and to maintain the required angle to the Sun that causes Earth's seasonal behaviour — not to mention the many other ways in which the Moon has been Earth's best friend. But one fact is certain — no matter how the Moon got to be what it is and where it is, the scientific consensus now is that its presence has been critical to our own existence. If the Moon wasn't pretty much exactly as it is, there would be no humans — in other words no sentient beings on our planet at all.

So, how would our planet look today if the Moon had not accompanied it on its journey around the Sun for so long? Now that astronomers and physicists have chosen to view our companion in space with more open eyes, most of them are willing to admit that Earth would have been completely different in almost every way.

The inescapable fact is that if it were not for the Moon's presence over the last four and a half billion years, the Earth would still be a half scorched, half frozen mass of rock, spinning crazily on its own axis; unstable to the point of frequently turning over, and with not the slightest hope of any life that did appear achieving anything more than a rudimentary presence before it was snuffed out — probably time and again.

Whilst the infant Earth did have a number of factors in its favour as a potential haven for simple life — most especially its position in the solar system — some of the most essential ingredients necessary for the development of advanced life were missing. One example of this is Earth's very fiery core. The large number of volcanoes that are present on the Earth's surface today bear testimony to the incredible temperatures that exist not too many kilometres below ground level. If volcanism ran rampant — as it would without the steadying influence of the Moon, virtually no life could exist, either on land or in the oceans. On the other hand, with the phenomenon known as plate tectonics in operation and volcanic activity evenly spread across the planet's surface, the red-hot material springing up from Earth's core provides the minerals and metals upon which life utterly depends for its existence.

It is probable that on other terrestrial type planets, such as Venus, there have been many occasions during which a solid and unremitting crust caused pressure to build so much within the hot core of the planet that when volcanism did take place, it was on a scale that remodelled the whole planetary surface. Even allowing for the fact that the surface of Venus is so hot, such events would undoubtedly destroy any life that was attempting to take hold.

One of the more obvious factors that makes our Moon so important to Earth is the tidal forces it exerts. Such forces are dependent on mass, and in comparison with the size of the Earth, the Moon is significant in its mass. There are moons in the solar system that are bigger and more massive than ours, but these are orbiting planets that are themselves many times larger than Earth. In terms of size proportionate to the planet around which it is spinning, our Moon is the most massive by far. The mass of our Moon has had a great bearing on the Earth as its close proximity means that it exerts around twice the pull of the Sun. The effect is particularly noticeable because Earth's surface is mostly covered with liquid water.

Every day as the Moon passes over the Earth its gravity tugs on the oceans, and in so doing it causes tides to rise and fall.

Since every action has an opposite and equal reaction, tidal forces also work on the side of the Earth away from the Moon, which is why most areas receive two high and low tides each day. Tides vary in height for several reasons. The shape of coastlines and depth due to continental shelves play a part but the major factor is the proximity of the Moon at any particular point in time, and also the relationship the Moon has to the Sun. This varies, and since the Sun also affects our tides, when the Moon and Sun are aligned or opposed (new Moon and full Moon) the tides will be particularly high.

Tides were crucial to the development of life in the oceans and were once much greater in force when the Moon was closer than it is today. In its early position it acted as a gravitational plough, ripping open Earth's crust each time it passed overhead, and spilling out the minerals and other substances that would be essential to life. These were then mixed into a giant mineral and metal soup thanks to the massive tides that tore across the young planet's surface.

Although it is now more distant from the Earth than it once was, the Moon still has a very significant part to play in the way sections of the Earth's surface constantly move around, redistributing volcanic activity and continuing the process of replenishing the minerals and metals present on the Earth's surface — a process that is so critical to the continuation of life. For those readers who wish to know more about the Moon's role in the way sections of the Earth's crust move around on the underlying mantle see Appendix 1 on plate tectonics.

One of the most important gifts that the Moon brought to the Earth was to control the way Earth spins on its axis. Before the Moon was present the Earth was spinning wildly and much faster than today. The tidal drag caused by the mass of the Moon has significantly calmed the once fierce spin of our planet. A vitally important consequence of this concerns weather. The infant Earth would have been a fearsome place, with constant epic storms and wind speeds beyond our comprehension if the Moon had not exerted its steadying influence.

Another effect of the Moon's presence was that it acted as a brake, gradually slowing down the rate of the spin of the Earth. As a natural consequence of the relationship of the two bodies, the Moon gradually began to move further and further away. This is still happening, and the surface-to-surface gap is increasing by just 3.8 cm (1.5 inches) per year. That means there has been a change of just 0.001% since modern humans emerged around 100,000 years ago.

The result of the gravity exchange between the two spheres also leads to a phenomenon known as 'tidal-lock', the effect of which has been to cause the Moon to always show the same face to the Earth. This occurrence is quite common with planetary satellites, and many other moons in the solar system behave in a similar way.

One of the most wonderful effects of the Moon's presence is how it has stabilised the Earth so that its angle of tilt relative to the Sun remains within a tight range. Known as 'obliquity' this angle oscillates between 22.1 and 24.5 degrees over a 41,000-year cycle. Right now, that angle is a mid-point 23.4°. It is this small range of angles that provides us with our all-important seasons.

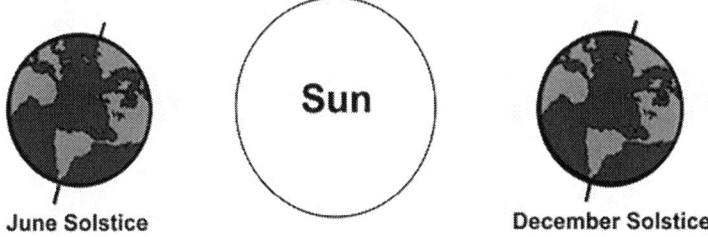

June Solstice   **December Solstice**

The natural angle of inclination of the planet means that at one part of its orbit the northern hemisphere is closer to the Sun, whereas in its opposite position relative to the Sun it is the southern hemisphere that is closest.

When seen in the diagram above, this angle does not look particularly significant, but it is enough to ensure an even and relatively precise warming of both hemispheres of the Earth throughout the year. If there were no such angle, the equatorial region of the Earth would be far hotter than it is now, whilst the poles would always be in semi-darkness and much colder than any part of the Earth under present circumstances.

In addition to its assistance in maintaining the current 23.4° angle of the Earth, the Moon serves another extremely significant function. The iron rich core of the Earth is colossally hot and extremely unstable. This means that in addition to turning on its axis the Earth also has a tendency to wobble.

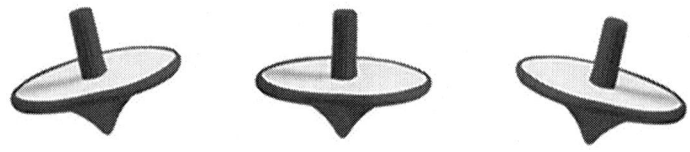

The Earth behaves like a spinning top, not only turning on its own axis but also wobbling as it does so.

The Earth is a dynamic object, and it wobbles in more than one way; some wobbles occurring over vast periods of time. It has been suggested that on some occasions prior to the presence of the Moon acting as a stabilising force, the Earth could have flipped over and started spinning in the opposite direction. If this were to have happened the repercussions on any emerging life would have been beyond catastrophic.

There is no longer any doubt that without the Moon, the situation of the Earth right now would be very different, and of course that also means that our own existence would not have been possible.

The bottom line is that the Moon has acted in a way that has made the Earth a perfect incubator to create a 'Garden of

Eden' — a planet that is suitable to sustain simple life and allow it to blossom to become truly intelligent. If our Moon fulfilled this role by pure accident of astronomical happenstance, it would be nothing less than a miracle. Despite the unfathomable hugeness of the universe, the chances of such a precise, complex series of events happening twice would surely be non-existent. But if it was a deliberate design, it could have been replicated any number of times across the entire cosmos.

Either we are alone, or the Moon is effectively a 'machine' deliberately designed to act upon the Earth and make it an incubator to nurture advanced, thinking life forms. And that conclusion is no longer a matter of debate because the manufacturer of the Moon went to 'astronomic' lengths to let us know what it had done.

We are at this point quite clear that there are three fundamental types of objects that are the pillars upon which all life on Earth rests: DNA, viruses, and the Moon. None of these could have arrived in any way other than deliberate design by the same entity several billion years ago.

Chapter Five

The Birth of a Moon

Even over four billion years after the solar system began to take shape, there is still a great deal of material passing back and forth amongst the planets that has not become permanently attached to or associated with any of the solar system's planets. Rogue asteroids of many different sorts from within the solar system itself are still common, as are comets and bodies that have entered the solar system from elsewhere. Even some established objects with orbits of their own would have been subjected to the almost constant game of interplanetary snooker that has been taking place for billions of years, and one of them could have been knocked from its orbit elsewhere and sent careering further into the solar system to be captured and subsequently take up residence as a moon around one of the planets.

It was once thought that this was the most likely explanation for Earth's Moon, and it was assumed that this 'visitor' to our part of space was captured by Earth's gravitational pull and became the Moon we know today.

All theories are subject to scientific testing and in the case of a captured companion it was our visits to the Moon itself that eventually made this theory far less likely than it had once appeared to be. This is because not only the American Apollo astronauts but also unmanned spacecraft have returned samples of Moon rock to Earth, which has been carefully analysed. One of the discoveries was that Moon rock has a great deal in common with Earth rock — to the extent that it seems certain that both planetary bodies developed at the same distance from the Sun. So however the Moon came into being, it was certainly not previously an entire body that came visiting and stayed on.

Bearing this in mind, even the most diehard exponents of the captured Moon theory were forced to admit that it eventually seemed not only unlikely but actually impossible.

Simultaneous Arrival

Another fairly early possible explanation for the presence of the Moon was known as the co-accretion theory and it suggested that both the Earth and the Moon formed from the disc of gas and heavier material that accumulated at the birth of the solar system in a band around the Sun at the distance where the Earth would eventually orbit. By pure chance when this material began to accrete — in other words to be drawn together under its own gravity to form larger clumps and then eventually whole planetary bodies, not one but two discreet bodies were formed. One was the Earth and the other was the Moon. The idea was that the Earth became gradually bigger, and the Moon eventually began to orbit the Earth. There was never any problem with this theory in terms of the similarity of material in both bodies, which was the main difficulty with the captured Moon idea, but there were significant other difficulties.

The biggest issue with the co-accretion theory is that it fails to explain the present angular momentum of the Moon and the way it travels around the Earth. This is a great problem, and accounts for the fact that this theory is not presently considered likely — or in fact possible.

The Giant Impact Hypothesis

By far the most popular potential explanation recently for how the Moon came to be what it is and where it is comes in the form of the 'giant impact hypothesis' — which assumes that a planet sized object slammed into the young Earth. Although this idea started out in a fairly simple form, it has been significantly analysed and looked at, so that now it appears in a number of different versions.

Originally it was suggested that a Mars sized body from elsewhere in the solar system had collided with the Earth. This theoretical body is usually named Theia, and it was suggested that its rocky composition was different, and probably not so robust as that of the Earth. Because of this, although Theia struck the Earth hard, the Earth itself remained largely intact, whilst Theia broke into fragments that eventually coalesced to make the Moon.

An alternative to this theory is that when Theia struck Earth, both planetary bodies were utterly destroyed and vaporised, and the components of both planets were thoroughly mixed, and that over time the extended arm of the disc of material became detached and coalesced into the Moon, whilst everything else formed the Earth.

Yet another version of this big whack theory seems to us to be the least likely because it demands two bodies that were almost identical in composition coming together. In this model, debris thrown out from the impact of Theia and the Earth coalesced into the Moon. What positively amazes us about this version of the hypothesis is that it seems to demand two discreet bodies, each with the same basic composition, sharing different parts of the same orbit around the Sun, and which eventually came together to create the impact. This far-fetched notion seems incredibly fanciful with the need for two virtually identical bodies sharing the same orbit for long enough to develop into fully fledged planets before meeting with an almighty crash.

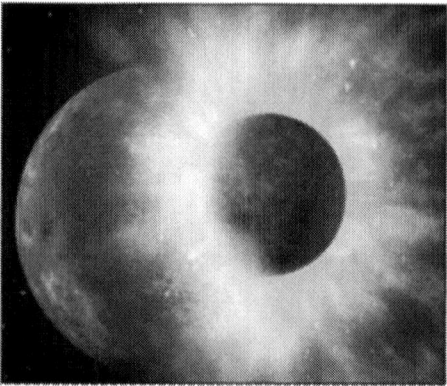

The giant impact hypothesis supposes that the planet Theia hit the Earth.

All versions of the giant impact theory have been subjected to hundreds of thousands of computer simulations, which these days can be carried out at lightning speed, and some versions of the theory hold up better than others. In all cases the nature of the impact, the direction from which it occurred, and the relative masses of the bodies in question have to be taken into account. All versions of this hypothesis deal well with the fact that Moon and Earth rocks have the same oxygen isotopes — and so therefore came into being at the same distance from the Sun, but significant problems remain when it comes to working out the Moon's angular momentum and the eventual spin speed of the Earth. At one point those working on the theory even went so far as to suggest that in order for things to work out as they did, a second large impact would have been necessary from the opposite direction — merely to try and explain how the Earth's rate spin is not a great deal faster than we see today.

At the time we wrote and published *Who Built the Moon?*, the theories itemised above were more or less the sum total of suggestions for the presence of the Moon, and particularly in the case of one or other version of the giant impact hypothesis it seemed that ever more bizarre modifications were having to be made to computer models in order to make this explanation work adequately.

Multi Extraterrestrial Impact Hypothesis

In 2017, twelve years after the publication of *Who Built the Moon?*, scientists in Israel took a step sideways in looking at the possible impact event, and came up with a new explanation as to how the Moon might have been created. It differed from the previous suggestion in one very important way, in that it did not rely on a single event but on a whole series of whacks which combined to create the Moon.

The 'Multi Extraterrestrial Impact Hypothesis' suggests that a succession of much smaller impacts on the Earth by unknown objects led to the presence of the Moon. Each individual strike of a rocky lump freed material from the surface of the Earth and caused a debris disc to form around the planet which quite quickly coalesced into a moonlet. The process would have been comparatively quick, and the first moonlet would have moved further from the Earth as the coalescing was taking place. There is an inference that this process took place during a period in which many loose meteorites and/or asteroids were invading our part of the solar system. As a result a second impact took place and another disc of material was formed, followed by the creation of another moonlet. The theory suggests that there may have been upwards of twenty such happenings, and that as the moonlets, one by one, reached a specific distance from the Earth, they came together to form ever larger bodies. The eventual result was Earth's Moon.

Many simulations were carried out by Professor Oded Aharonson and Dr Raluca Rufu from the Department of Earth and Planetary Sciences at the Weizmann Institute of Science in Rehovot, Israel, and they eventually put forward a paper explaining their research.

According to Aharonson and Rufu the theory worked well in the simulations and went a long way towards solving problems with the giant impact models for the Moon's creation. This mechanism would have left us with a Moon that was indeed very similar in rock type to that of the Earth, and at the same time because of the mechanisms involved would account for the fact that although the Moon's composition is very similar to that of the Earth it is much lighter overall in mass. This is because the heavier rocks and metals from the impactors would have been left on the Earth, whilst material removed from the Earth would have been lightweight, surface rock and not heavier rocks or minerals from lower down in the Earth's crust.

The scientists who carried out these simulations came to the conclusion that the Multi Extraterrestrial Impact Hypothesis also explained how the infant Earth, which would originally have been spinning extremely quickly on its axis, was slowed, thanks, as they said, "to an effective draining of angular momentum from the target's initial spin due to the often-neglected angular momentum carried by escaping mass." In addition, they concluded that their model demonstrated possible changes in axial rotation of the Earth due to the repeated impacts.

There is no doubt that had this multi-missile theory existed at the time we researched and wrote *Who Built the Moon?* we would have paid special attention to it. It was and remains our own theory that the Moon was deliberately engineered in order to carry out the functions for the Earth that it does so unerringly on a daily basis. What this hypothesis appears to be, especially if it was carried out deliberately, is a form of 'sculpture', albeit on a massive scale, that would allow for a controlled building of the Moon, taking account of its intended size and mass. If an intelligent agency was part of the scenario, with the option to make necessary changes with each successive impact — much like the individual chisel strikes of an artist creating a sculpture from stone, this would allow a 'fineness of touch' that could never have been the case with any giant impact.

It would obviously have required massive forces to be harnessed, and probably over a long period of time. Nevertheless we return to our comments in *Who Built the Moon?* "Engineering is just engineering". It matters little whether one is building a car or a moon. A plan is made and is carried out. Of course to even contemplate any engineering project depends on the ability of those involved to be in a position to achieve the objectives they are setting themselves. As an example, the all-round 15th century Italian genius Leonardo da Vinci theorised about all manner of machines, including the helicopter. His mind was great enough to address the mathematical and physical problems involved but the society in which he lived had not advanced sufficiently to provide the 'means' for achieving the objective. This was clearly not the case in terms of the engineers of the Moon. Not only was the notion and the blueprint possible but the machinery and technical expertise necessary to achieve the objective must also have been present. We might find this to be amazing but it is no more impossible than any of Leonardo's dreams — the reality of which are now almost everywhere we look.

At the time we wrote *Who Built the Moon?* none of the theories then present regarding how the Moon came to be orbiting the Earth fitted especially well with our hypothesis that the Moon must have been deliberately engineered. What we little expected at that time was for someone, or in this case a group of people, to come along within a few years and to offer a means for creating the Moon.

Where Did the Impactors Come From?

A question that might be asked regarding the Multi Extraterrestrial Impact Hypothesis of the Moon's creation is, why did so many strikes by passing asteroids or meteorites take place in such a comparatively short space of time in order to serve the hypothesis? The Earth does not appear to be as covered with impact craters as bodies such as the Moon or Mars but there is a good reason for this. The geology of the Earth is dynamic, with a surface that is constantly changing thanks to volcanism and the ever-shifting surface we call continental drift. Also a large percentage of the Earth's surface is covered in water and impact craters at the bottom of the oceans would be far from obvious.

Nevertheless, the Earth has been struck regularly during the billions of years it has existed and many of the impacts would have been extremely large, but we have to also bear in mind that this is, thankfully, not a regular event. This might cause us to pause and wonder how so many opportune strikes by extraterrestrial bodies could have contributed to the hammering of the young Earth and therefore to the presence of the Moon?

If our hypothesis is correct and if the Moon was deliberately planned and engineered, the presence of the objects that impacted the Earth in order to create the Moon is not really a puzzle at all. No matter how hard it might be for some people to swallow, the truth is that the objects in question must have been brought to our part of the solar system from somewhere else, in order to serve the needs of the project. Even if the multiple strike idea had existed when we wrote *Who Built the Moon?* we might have had to stretch our minds to try and establish where the very specific ammunition used had been sourced, but that was before NASA sent its spacecraft Dawn to the asteroid belt and in particular to the minor planet Ceres.

The asteroid belt is a region of space between the orbits of the planets Mars and Jupiter which is filled with a million or more pieces of rock, some of which are large but the majority very small. This belt of rocky debris orbits the Sun in more or less the way a planet would. This is why when this zone of debris was first recognised it was thought that it may once have been a planet, perhaps very much like the Earth or Mars, and that it had somehow been destroyed. Later astronomers began to believe that because there was nowhere near enough material in the asteroid belt to have ever represented even a small terrestrial type planet, there never had been a planet in this position and that such a body had failed to coalesce because of the proximity of giant Jupiter with its massive gravity. However, orbiting within the asteroid belt is a strange and truly alien minor planet which came to be called Ceres, which is radically different in nature and composition to anything else in the asteroid belt.

As we will presently see, the origin of the impactors that were used to build the Moon is now no mystery at all, and what is more it has become obvious that an entire planet was destroyed in order to obtain them. For many years the idea that a full-size terrestrial planet existed between the orbit of Mars and Jupiter had been taken seriously but later it became discounted as being nothing more than a myth. However, Ceres is exactly in the location where the notional planet Phaeton was predicted to be according to something known as the Titius-Bode Law, which turns out to be extremely significant.

The Titius-Bode law is a formula that predicts where the planets of the solar system are likely to orbit, working outwards from the Sun. Although it is quite complex, put simply the Titius-Bode Law describes where each successive planet will naturally orbit — at a distance twice as great as the previous planet. The law is named after the 18th century astronomers, Johann Daniel Titius and Johan Elert Bode, who noted the positions of the inner planets and the closest of the gas giants. The law works well in the case of the first four planets from Mercury to Mars but then there is a conspicuous gap until the law takes over again with the planet Jupiter. Like a missing tooth in a broad smile this law states that there should have been a substantial planet at the point where tiny Ceres was found by Giuseppe Piazza in 1801. Because there is not a terrestrial planet in this location astronomers decided that the law must be faulty.

Then in 1913 a British astronomer by the name of Mary Blagg carried out a highly detailed Fourier analysis of Bode's Law, which identified a significant flaw in the original concept which, when corrected, gave it a reborn credibility. Unfortunately (but typically for new and unwanted information) her paper was largely ignored at the time and it lay forgotten for forty years before it came to light again in 1953. Suddenly it was found that her predictions had been validated by discoveries of new planetary satellites unknown at the time of the original publication. The proof of any theory is to have predictions confirmed by later data, and so there are solid astronomical calculations that tell us that there should be a Mars sized planet where tiny Ceres now sits. All of the evidence points to the planet Phaeton being a super-ancient reality which became the source of a series of projectiles that sculpted the Earth and created the Moon. Of course, the astronomical authorities will not discuss this issue publicly, because they would have to consider the cause of this genuinely world-changing, hugely beneficial event. There are no logical reasons as to how or why it would have happened as a random natural disintegration of a planet that just happened to impact the young Earth. And they are certainly disinclined to be seen to consider that it could have been the result of cosmic engineering by an unknown intelligence.

The truth is that there is very good reason to believe that the principles of the Titius-Bode Law do indeed hold good, and that the tiny planet called Ceres is a place marker for the original major planet known in legend as Phaeton.

Chapter Six

The Oxygen Engineers

Our contention is that our home planet was deliberately remodelled — together with its orbiting counter-balancing moon, to prepare it for the seeding of the self-replicating, ever evolving life modules we call DNA. Whoever, or whatever, conducted this program of the cultivation of future intelligence had a clear plan as to how things would unfold. And, as we will go on to demonstrate, this entity has left a detailed message to confirm the way it proceeded. However, we first need to consider just how magnificent the planning was to ensure that the seeded life would blossom in exactly the planned way over many eons.

Whilst Darwin's Theory of Evolution is generally accepted as being broadly correct, it does have many significant shortcomings as a description of how species undergo wholesale change. There have been periods in the past during which massive about-turns have occurred, such as the sudden ending of the entire category of creatures we have generically named 'dinosaurs'. Some of these lizard like, egg layers were amazingly massive for land based creatures, straining the boundary between the limitations of bone and muscle structures against the power of Earth's gravity. Perhaps they were always an evolutionary cul-de-sac and they all but disappeared in a handful of years following a major impact event that produced something like a sunless nuclear winter. Of course life's excursion into the realms of these fantastic creatures was not wasted because some of the smaller versions of these dinosaurs survived to become the birds we see today — which are so integral to the fertilisation process of so many plants that feed us and other species.

Like the larger dinosaurs, human beings have also come close to the edge of extinction on occasions in the past in what are termed 'bottleneck' events, when numbers have dwindled to a very few individuals. A recent bottleneck happened only 74,000 years ago when an eruption of a supervolcano occurred at the site of what is now Lake Toba in Indonesia. The Toba catastrophe is believed to have caused a global volcanic winter of six to ten years followed by 1000 years of colder seasons. Today, the Earth's surface remains quite delicate in places like Indonesia's 'Ring of Fire' and North America's Yellowstone Park, where the ground regularly rises and subsides. Fortunately this tendency has been trending downward in recent years. Thankfully experts suggest there are no concerns of an impending volcanic eruption in this particular location at least!

Over the very long term, however, the surface of the Earth is constantly being remade and remoulded. Our planet is a very dynamic place where the forces of plate tectonics ensure that old surface material is subsumed, and new material appears elsewhere. Mountain ranges, formed as a result of plate tectonics, are eventually subject to weathering, which gradually flattens them, as streams and rivers carry their life-giving soil and nutrients to lower areas and ultimately to the sea. Right now the collision between the continental plate on which India sits is still in the process of crashing into the main Asian plate, heading northwards by 5 cm (2 inches) a year and causing parts of the Himalayas to increase in height by around 10 mm each year.

In colder regions glaciers move fantastic amounts of material around, whilst the volcanic activity, ultimately inspired by the process of plate tectonics, has played its own part in forming the landscapes that are familiar today. The fact is that it would be very difficult now to find any large parts of the Earth's surface that have endured for more than a few million years. But there are exceptions and one of these is Australia. As incredible as it may seem, there are rocks in Australia that are at least three billion years old and zircon crystals are present in the Jack Hills of mid Western Australia that are an amazing 4.375 billion years old, which means these particular rocks were present very shortly after the Earth formed.

Also in Australia is to be found at least one life form that has not evolved one jot since it suddenly appeared on the surface of our infant planet.

This is astonishing. Whilst some of these same super-ancient life forms went on to evolve into everything we see today, from daisies to blue whales and of course to humans, these indigenous Australian bacteria remained completely unchanged!

Basically, and it might seem somewhat mysteriously, the DNA code built into some of these tiny creatures to be found in Australia has forbidden any variation to their composition, so they remain frozen in time. This makes them unique because everything else that came from early bacteria, and which did permit changes, has been lost to the eons of the distant past. New species arrived, evolved and mostly disappeared as failed experiments, and only the most successful survived. All life forms on Earth today are descendants of the 'change permitting' variety of cyanobacteria, and as a result everything is closely related; so that bananas for example have 44.1% of their genetic make-up in common with us humans.

The Hamelin Pool stromatolites of Western Australia are mounds of limestone that were and are still created by these cyanobacteria. Layer by slow layer across a fantastic timescale these incredibly small bacteria have lived and died, leaving behind their remains, which gradually harden. If left undisturbed the stromatolites simply keep growing, though at an incredibly slow rate.

It is estimated that the stromatolites of Hamelin Pool are at least 3.5 billion years old, and nobody knows for sure whether the same sort of cyanobacteria that made them put in an appearance any earlier on other parts of the planet because so few truly ancient stromatolites have survived the ravages of our extremely reactive and ever-changing world.

At the time when the first cyanobacteria were forming the stromatolites at Hamelin Pool the atmosphere of the Earth was largely made up of carbon dioxide, alongside water vapour, ammonia, and methane: not dissimilar to the atmosphere of Mars today. It goes without saying that such a mixture would be lethally poisonous to any higher life form. At that time the Earth was still spinning on its axis around 30% faster than today, so that there were 18 hours in a day. The Moon was also much closer to the Earth than it is during our era, leading to tremendous upheavals each time the Moon passed overhead, and adding to a hellish environment in which it is hard to believe that any form of life could possibly have survived — and yet the stromatolites of Western Australia exist to prove conclusively that somehow it did.

The stromatolites are the evidence of all the cyanobacteria that lived and died in this place, and as lowly and diminutive as they are, the cyanobacteria that so slowly built this limestone that is their legacy probably rank as the most important expression of life that has ever existed. Cyanobacteria are unicellular microorganisms, measuring between 0.5 and 100 micrometres; from invisibly small up to the width of a human hair. Cyanobacteria (Cyan means blue-green) are photosynthetic, which means they absorb sunlight and excrete oxygen as part of their life cycle. Basically they 'eat' sunlight and 'pooh' oxygen. This makes them tiny engines of transformation, using energy radiated from the Sun to create the life-enabling gas, oxygen — which makes up around 21% of our current atmosphere.

Not all bacteria do this but the fact that cyanobacteria do has probably been the most important single factor on the long road that ultimately led to the appearance of our own species. It is thought that the existence of cyanobacteria ultimately led to more refined forms of photosynthesis as seen in plants, a process which keeps the Earth's atmosphere oxygen rich, though blue-green algae in our oceans, which is composed of cyanobacteria, still supplies our atmosphere with far more oxygen than all the trees and other green plants combined. This means the experiment in the very simplest form of photosynthesis that was already in operation three and a half billion years ago is still taking place. Much of the oxygen in our atmosphere today is also provided by phytoplankton, free floating and usually minute organisms in our oceans that stand at the base of aquatic food chains and which themselves, like us, ultimately owe their existence to cyanobacteria. However, despite these later exponents of photosynthesis, cyanobacteria themselves are as important to us today as they were so long ago.

All higher life forms such as our own species are completely dependent on oxygen, the by-product of photosynthesis. Oxygen is an element that is too chemically reactive to remain as a free element in air without being constantly replaced by the photosynthesis that is taking place all around us. The organisms that survive by photosynthesis and which create the oxygen upon which the world depends are nowhere near as complex as the higher life forms that breathe oxygen. The first creatures that inhaled oxygen are thought to have appeared around 3.1 billion years ago. This was around 500 million years before what was known as the Great Oxidization Event, sometimes termed more descriptively as the Great Oxidization Revolution.

At this time the masses of microscopic self-replicating oxygen engines we call cyanobacteria became too successful for some early evolving varieties. The numbers of oxygen makers grew so huge that vast amounts of the gas were pumped into the atmosphere, causing a mass extinction of many early life forms to which oxygen was as good as a poison. It is thought by many experts that this was a phase-change event in evolution, when there was a rapid clearing of the old, 'simple' life forms, allowing space for the advancement of multicellular organisms, which relied totally on oxygen for respiration, and which ultimately led to our own ancestry.

The life cycle of cyanobacteria and later photosynthetic species ensured that the atmosphere of the Earth would be radically different than that of any of the other terrestrial type planets in the solar system. The presence of oxygen in such quantities had implications beyond simply allowing higher life forms to evolve; it gave them the means to eventually dominate our planet. Oxygen is essential in order for combustion to take place in our atmosphere — and this fact has been crucial to the rise of our own species. By controlling fire, early humans could spread into colder environments, where they could both keep warm and cook food. Fire assisted in the making of tools prior to metallurgy but once smelting was understood a whole new world opened up for humanity. A great many of the advances that made humanity what it is today came courtesy of an understanding and manipulation of metallurgy, and this would have been impossible in an oxygen low atmosphere. Humanity could and did survive without metal but all advanced technology relies on it, as metal cannot be manipulated except under the extreme temperatures that are reliant upon oxygen. It is hard to believe that any advanced civilization could exist that was not oxygen breathing and oxygen reliant in numerous other ways.

No other planet that we know of has such a preponderance of oxygen.

The oxygen we breathe is entirely due to the presence of DNA based creatures. If we, and a host of serious scientific thinkers, are right and these early bacteria were the result of 'Directed Panspermia' by an Unknown Creative Agency, there had to be a long-term plan rather than a quick spray of 'life seeds'.

The entity we have named the UCA that was responsible for singling out the Earth for special treatment did not simply provide the right circumstances for life to take hold and survive. It went much, much further.

Having created the perfect environment within which different forms of life could eventually flourish it remained necessary to place several colonies of the essential bacteria upon the Earth and thereby to give life the kick-start it required. But the many steps required that would lead to intelligent creatures would be complex, and required supervision across billions of years.

Herein lay the genius of the enterprise. Many of these earliest forms of life not only had the possibility within them to advance and gradually create more sophisticated species, they were themselves the tools by which the whole of the Earth would continue to terraform itself into the ultimate desired environment so that it could accommodate the higher forms of life that were to come. The task was far from finished as the Moon began to slowly retreat from the Earth, and the planet settled into its controlled angle of inclination relative to its orbit around the Sun. What the UCA had achieved at this stage was merely the precursor — a means of setting the stage for the magnificent production that was to follow.

The noxious environment that was on offer to the first cyanobacteria suited it well, and it became part of a two-stage process. These tiny self-replicating machines begat adjusted versions of themselves, of a kind that flourished in the sort of atmosphere one might find today on Mars. Entities that relished a high carbon dioxide environment positively exploded into success, especially in the Earth's shallow oceans. There, for millions of years, they grew, with occasional changes during cell replication leading to even more successful species, though it appears that it had been planned from the start that a proportion of these carbon dioxide dependent life forms would ultimately breed themselves out of existence.

So it was, 2.4 billion years ago that oxygen levels in Earth's atmosphere had become so great that the entities that had provided the oxygen started to be killed by the very gas that they had been creating. This hinge-point in the history of the Earth caused a swing into the next stage in the advancement of life to take place. Somehow, surviving in areas where oxygen had accumulated, new creatures had emerged that were eking out a living in a very different way. They were multicellular, and instead of 'creating' oxygen, these more advanced forms were now consuming it. So it was that vast amounts of the more advanced carbon dioxide dependent creatures died out in a very short period of time, leaving behind them others of their kind that were more adaptable but opening up space for oxygen breathing species.

Ultimately, some sort of balance was achieved. Cyanobacteria and later plants provided oxygen as a part of their life cycle, whilst oxygen breathing creatures turned that oxygen back into carbon dioxide.

Little by little, conditions on the Earth, created and constantly modified by the preprogrammed life forms, led to a massive spurt forward in increasingly sophisticated creatures. Species came and went but the train rolled on relentlessly towards a form of life that did much more than simply survive and reproduce: It thought!

The scene had been set by what must have been a programmed change to create a world with a permanently replenished oxygen rich atmosphere. This shift in emphasis from 'sunlight engines' to 'oxygen engines' allowed for the evolution of creatures that were mobile and able to use tools. The atmosphere had become ideal for fire, the essential ingredient for the eventual manufacture of glass, ceramics, and metals — the ingredients necessary for an advanced civilization and concepts like space flight.

Chapter Seven

How Fact Can Emulate Fiction

As we intimated in Chapter 1, NASA's Dawn Mission to Ceres appears to have changed the organization's attitude to extraterrestrials, coinciding as it did with its decision to openly look for signs of intelligent life outside of our home planet. Supporting the 'needle-in-a-haystack' deep space efforts by the likes of SETI is one thing, but to acknowledge that the potential for 'technosignatures' (evidence of alien activities in our local vicinity) might exist was indeed a revolutionary step-change. For a number of reasons we could not believe that this significant alteration in attitude regarding alien life by NASA and the reinvigorated Dawn mission were merely coincidental.

We had to ask ourselves the questions: Why had the Dawn mission apparently been shelved and then suddenly taken up again in around 2005, and why was the mission to Ceres extended whilst Dawn was orbiting the minor planet when it was always intended that if the spacecraft was behaving well it should be sent to a further target in the asteroid belt? We felt that there was something NASA was not talking about in a public sense — information that it had at its disposal or which it might even have gained as a result of our book *Who Built the Moon?* Our own minds were turning in the direction of the minor planet Ceres in the months after publication, and it seems a possibility that something in our book could have brought the significance of the Dawn mission back into focus around 2005 as far as NASA was concerned. In particular, as we watched the mission unfold, it appeared that NASA was looking for something — but something about which it was remaining deliberately silent.

In order to explain why at least some agencies within NASA might have become excited by Dawn's visit to Ceres, we need to go back in time to a story that was written over seventy years ago.

In 1948 the British writer and science fanatic Arthur C. Clarke wrote a short story with the title of "Sentinel of Eternity", which was published in the spring of 1951 in a magazine entitled *10 Story Fantasy*. The story proved popular and went on to be republished in other magazines in the years that followed. "Sentinel of Eternity" was only a few pages in length, but it was fascinating enough to convince movie director Stanley Kubrick that it might be the basis of an interesting and thought-provoking movie. He met Arthur C. Clarke and the cooperation began which led eventually to the epic *2001: A Space Odyssey*, which was released in 1968 and became one of the greatest movies of all time.

The original work, "Sentinel of Eternity", is set in a mythical present and is the story of a geologist working with colleagues on the surface of the Moon when they discover a large, pyramidal object of unknown composition but something which is obviously not a naturally occurring structure. In the story the incredible importance of this object, which Clarke calls 'the Sentinel', is that it is proof positive of intelligent life beyond the Earth. It could not have been built by humanity. The reader never learns in the narrative precisely what the Sentinel is — or anything relating to the culture that created it. The Sentinel is made of some super tough crystalline substance; it makes no sound, carries no markings, and defies every attempt to gain access to it until eventually it is utterly destroyed in a nuclear detonation employed to try and gain access to it. The geologist telling the first-person story makes the suggestion that the Sentinel was probably put in place, maybe eons before, by a culture that could have originated many light years from Earth, and that it might be one of many such structures left in places where advanced life was likely to occur. It is possible, he tells the reader, that the destruction of the Sentinel will alert the aliens, wherever they may be, to the fact that intelligent life has indeed developed in this particular part of our galaxy and that it has achieved at least local space flight. He suggests that, woken to the readiness of humanity to take its next step, the aliens who created the Sentinel may soon return.

We are astonished that Arthur C. Clarke conceived the story of the Sentinel because it turned out to be so accurate. Clarke was a great scientific thinker, and he must have asked himself the question: "If I was an advanced alien who introduced intelligent life to the Earth, how would I communicate the fact to the resulting species once it was advanced enough to be capable of space flight?" He concluded that he would put a trigger on the Moon that would point to the 'real' history of humanity. As we would discover, it was Arthur C. Clarke's further suggestion in the movie *2001: A Space Odyssey* that this object on the Moon would send a signal to another solar system body, where the real truth of Earth's history could be found. There it would be safe from the turbulent and ever-changing nature of the Earth itself, or its peculiar and extremely vulnerable Moon.

We will demonstrate that there was actually no Sentinel on the lunar surface, and that the Moon itself is the trigger to the safeguarded knowledge. No object is necessary amidst the lunar dust because the truth of the situation is written into the Moon itself as a result of its size, its mass, and its orbital characteristics — though in this way the Moon is every bit as much a Sentinel as the object Clarke's character found on its surface.

Arthur C. Clarke died in 2008, so it was not possible for us to quiz him regarding what was going through his mind when he penned the story, but we have often wondered whether he was party to some of the facts regarding the Moon that informed our own work. Although we might be the first researchers and writers to publish a book identifying the fact that the Moon cannot be a natural object, all the information that was available to us and which led to our book exists in plain sight; it is not difficult to recognise or particularly complicated to unravel, but at the same time it is incredibly unlikely for anyone to detect an entry point into this multifaceted conundrum. As it turned out we got lucky! We have never suggested that we are the first to recognise all the utterly improbable patterns written into the Earth–Moon and Moon–Sun relationships — but we were the first to piece them all together, and this had come about because of the particular and peculiar circumstances of our researches into ancient geodetic metrology.

Arthur C. Clarke made a point of only using material for his science fiction stories and movies that he considered plausible within the confines of what was understood at the time. He was also on very good terms with any number of astronomers, physicists, and other scientists, and may have been party to information these people possessed but about which they were unwilling or forbidden to share in a public forum. Taking everything into account it seems almost certain to us that Clarke knew how extremely unlikely the Moon is as a naturally occurring object, and that the Sentinel was a method of expressing his knowledge and suspicions regarding matters he was unwilling to put into print in a direct sense at the time.

It is obvious to anyone who has read "Sentinel of Eternity" and who has also seen *2001: A Space Odyssey*, or read the subsequent book, that the two stories are intimately related. The pyramidal Sentinel of the earlier story becomes a black obelisk in the movie but as with the Sentinel, it is found on the Moon. However, at its commencement the movie shows a scenario set long ago, at the time of the divide between hominids as an advanced ape and their transition into modern humans. It is at this stage that the obelisk first appears to one of the ape hominids, instilling the creature with qualities of reasoning and adaptability that it had not previously possessed.

The discovery of the obelisk buried on the Moon, a million and more years after the hominid sequence, marks the next stage in the advancement of humanity. After this the movie takes us on a journey aboard an interplanetary space mission that is headed to the region of Jupiter. There are adventures on the way but the next sighting of the obelisk — and therefore the next stage in the advancement of humanity, takes place close to the region of space where the minor planet Ceres is to be found. Without explaining the whole storyline of *2001: A Space Odyssey* (which incidentally has quite definitely stood the test of time and is well worth watching), we wonder what specifically connected the Earth, where the obelisk was first seen, the Moon, and then this particular region of space in the mind of Arthur C. Clarke? We came to understand that the connection must be the tiny planet Ceres because the obelisk appears in both locations, and in the story the obelisk is an allegorical representation of the Moon itself and almost certainly also Ceres. In each case it represents the next stage in the advancement of humanity as laid out by the makers of the Moon.

Could it be that when the Dawn mission was underway, some agencies at NASA were expecting or at least hoping to find 'something' on the surface of Ceres that might confirm beliefs they already held about extraterrestrial visitors such as those we have designated the UCA? What makes this seem entirely likely is that by the time Dawn was launched, humanity's understanding of the surface of the Moon was extensive. There was hardly a square kilometre of the Moon that had not been scanned, examined, and mapped. Apparently nothing of extraterrestrial origin has been found on the Moon — even though NASA seems to have had good reason to expect that some object of alien origin would be present. It is quite possible that this being the case, and that eventually possessed of the knowledge of the true significance of Ceres, NASA turned its attention in that direction. The surface of little Ceres was examined in the greatest detail by Dawn, which overflew the little planet in every conceivable direction. Sadly for NASA it seems certain that those who conducted the search for 'something' on the tiny planet's surface were just as disappointed in the case of Ceres as they had been regarding the Moon. What they had apparently failed to realise is that there was no object on the surface of either body that confirmed an alien visit, and this for a couple of very good reasons.

The chances of any object, no matter how resilient, being able to stand the test of time on any planetary surface for up to three billion years would be less than negligible. In the case of the Moon, it is immediately obvious with the most cursory glance that it has been battered and pummelled by any number of meteorite strikes. The Moon has no significant atmosphere and so cannot protect itself in the way the Earth does. Incoming objects do not burn up as they approach the Moon, which makes it especially vulnerable. To leave any structure on the surface of the Moon would be to risk it being squashed flat at any moment. Meanwhile, any object left on the surface of Ceres would be even less likely to survive. A close-up analysis of the planet eventually showed that almost anything placed upon its surface, like the meteorites that sometimes strike it, would be sucked down into the soft body of Ceres and would soon disappear for good.

As we will presently see, as an epitaph to what the UCA achieved in our part of the solar system, and in terms of what it did regarding the destruction of an entire planet, the Moon itself and also Ceres were the structures that remained as proof of what had taken place. Both could be certain to survive the ravages of such a colossal period of time, and both carried mathematical evidence of their origins. Working forward from this, any further information the UCA had wished to leave us had to be left elsewhere and kept safe in ways other than those that applied to either the Moon or Ceres.

There must have been some very disappointed individuals at NASA on the day Dawn fell silent, but if so, that was because they had failed to understand the ingenuity of the UCA. They had been looking for some tangible evidence of all that had taken place in our solar system so long ago, and for a possible message from the agency that was responsible. That message does exist, but the agencies at NASA who searched for material proof failed to understand the utterly inclusive nature of the terraforming that had taken place.

Apart from some changes in its attitude, NASA remains generally silent on the subject of the connection between the Moon and Ceres that we are about to explain, and meanwhile SETI goes on burning huge budgets to listen out for a radio broadcast that has almost certainly never been sent. But if such an eventuality did occur, what would SETI want to hear? What is the sort of message that would make SETI turn its receivers up to full and convince it that it had really picked up a message from an alien source?

As we mentioned, the unmanned spacecraft Voyagers 1 and 2 had immediate missions of investigation of some of our neighbours in the Sun's family, but it was intended that the Voyagers would eventually leave the solar system and carry on into interstellar space — probably indefinitely. Currently Voyager 1 is zipping along at an impressive 17 kilometres every second — that is 38,000 miles per hour.

It was decided that the Voyagers should carry messages, so that if against all the odds they were picked up by an alien culture they could provide an introduction to the Earth and to humans. The craft carried a plaque, which attempted to show where the Earth was in relation to a number of pulsars, which aliens might recognise, and they each also carried a gold plated copper disc, similar to a vinyl record, with a collection of sounds and music from various cultures.

All very nice, but seemingly somewhat 'antiquated' by today's methods of communication, though it does show how much technology moves on in half a century, let alone the 75,000 years it would take a Voyager craft to reach the nearest star — even if it were travelling in a straight line.

What the Voyagers did not have on board is a message written specifically in mathematics, which is a shame because these days most scientific agencies agree that the best way to communicate with any alien culture that might exist would be by using something that would be meaningful to all technological life forms, which of course could only mean the language of mathematics. It is odd that the Voyagers did not carry specifically created mathematical messages because the famous astrophysicist Carl Sagan was heavily involved with the creation of the message aboard both craft, and he was also the author of the novel *Contact* that was first published just eight years later. In this book Sagan 'did' hypothesise about the use of mathematics as the universal language of intergalactic contact.

In his novel, Carl Sagan describes a fictional alien message buried deep inside the numerical representation of the transcendental number π, the ratio of the diameter of a circle to its circumference, and it is perhaps the most fundamental value in the entire universe. It is a little over the number 3 being 3.1416 to four decimal places, but there is a stream of digits after the decimal point that apparently tumble on randomly for ever. π otherwise expressed as pi is the most inclusive ratio there is and would be recognised anywhere, meaning it would be a natural choice for any entity or culture wishing to make a 'handshake' contact with an alien life form. 'Speaking' pi is a true and certain sign to connect sentient life forms across any amount of time and space.

Chapter Eight

The Message in the Machine

In Arthur C. Clarke's fictional account of an unknown alien origin regarding our own intellectual development the author made it plain that there was a need for humans to become aware of their benefactor so that humanity could move on to another level of development. This is a key point in Clarke's story — and also a key point in terms of the actual events we have uncovered.

The idea of directed panspermia (the theory that life on Earth developed as a result of the deliberate intervention of a third party from elsewhere in the Cosmos) is not only a respectable theory; it is the 'only' conceivable explanation for life existing on Earth once all clearly false theories have been swept away. But surely it would have been entirely understandable if the entity we call the Unknown Creative Agency (UCA) had engineered the Earth, assembled the Moon, sprayed our warm, little planet with bacteria containing beautifully programmed DNA, and then moved along to the next suitable solar system to repeat its altruistic feat of seeding life. In fact our evidence shows that this was not what happened, and it has become apparent to us that in the case of the Earth the UCA went to extraordinary lengths to make sure that an intelligent species developing upon the planet would realise what it had done. We can therefore be in little doubt that there must be a message of unparalleled importance waiting to be received, understood, and acted upon.

The reality is that we have at our disposal an extremely clear message that the operatives at SETI would jump at in a heartbeat, if only they were not totally fixated on the strangely simplistic idea that any incoming communication must be transmitted by means of the 19th century concept of radio signals. Just as the Voyager mission planners thought a gold plated 'vinyl disc' was the height of modernity for intergalactic correspondence, SETI seems to have a spectacularly myopic view of the cosmos and its potential inhabitants, though to be fair to SETI, it is simply spending its money on what its operatives consider to be their best guess at a medium that 'might' be used for an incoming call. As we have already stated, we doubt that the teams at SETI have any real idea of what they are looking for or what any message received would either look like or be intended to achieve.

The reality is that at least the first part of the message has already been delivered, and it explains exactly what the UCA did to engineer the 'life support machine' we call the Earth. This is beyond doubt. But there are extremely good reasons to expect that beyond the fantastic information regarding the true origins of the Earth and its life, which is present for absolutely anyone to see, there is also a further, highly complex, and world-changing message waiting to be opened.

The Measure of the Worlds

We believe that Oded Aharonson and Raluca Rufu of the Department of Earth and Planetary Sciences at the Weizmann Institute of Science in Israel have, so to speak, 'hit the nail on the head' with their multiple Earth impact explanation for the existence of the Moon. The now missing planet Phaeton, which once orbited the Sun between the planets Mars and Jupiter, was broken up and giant chunks of the resulting debris were fired at the Earth, possibly using Mars as a centrifugal slingshot. Multiple impacts were used over a relatively short period of time to produce a cloud of debris that would form the Moon and also sculpt the Earth so that the dimensions and relative mass of both the Earth and the Moon would create the desired incubator and, importantly, tell the resulting intelligent life form precisely what had been done.

The remains of the donor planet Phaeton became the asteroid belt, and different material was brought from elsewhere (most likely from a dead comet) to create the little planet Ceres, which was placed in the asteroid belt but which was so strange in composition that it clearly had to be an 'outsider'. Ceres together with the Moon and the Earth were all shaped to a precise plan, but the one fixed object that the UCA could not alter in this incredible engineering feat was the Sun. Even for a super-advanced entity like the UCA, the size and mass of the star at the centre of our then young solar system was an immutable fact. As a result the Sun had to become the UCA's reference point; in other words the Sun is the object that the Earth, Moon, and Ceres can be measured against.

The UCA ensured that the Earth it engineered ended up with a circumference that was precisely 109.288 times smaller than that of the Sun. Of course, 1 in 109.288 sounds like a rather unimportant, arbitrary value — but it is not. This ratio introduces us to a number that appears time and again with regard to the relationships of the Sun, the Earth, the Moon, and Ceres. In this case we can see that in terms of the length of its circumference, one quadrant of the Sun is equal to the circumference of 27.322 Earths.

In this way the UCA also ensured that the Moon would be 27.322% the size of the Earth.

The UCA also designed the motion of the Moon in such a way that at the time when intelligent life on Earth reached maturity (right now) each of the Moon's orbits around our planet would take a neat 27.322 Earth days.

These are in no way the only examples when the pivotal number 27.322 appears in terms of the relationship of these particular bodies. It is important to stress that the number 27.322 appears in all manner of apparently unrelated ways, for example as we have seen as percentages, but also with regard to the sizes of the bodies in question, their orbital characteristics, and their mass values. Surely this repeated, always very precise value must have some meaning? As a potential coincidence the constant appearance of 27.322 is off the scale — way off the scale! (Readers may wish to look at the table in Appendix 2 in order to appreciate just how popular the number 27.322 actually is in our neck of the solar system.)

It can also be observed that the builder conspired to ensure that the Moon has a circumference that is a very neat 400 times smaller than the Sun, and that at the present time (when we have sufficient intelligence to register the fact) the Moon orbits the Earth at 1/400th of the distance between the Earth and the Sun. This is also clearly no coincidence, and it is very important in terms of the 'apparent' interaction of the Moon and the Sun as seen from Earth. It is the size of the Moon relative to that of the Sun, together with the distance of the Moon's orbit around the Earth, that allows full solar eclipses to take place. These occurrences are extremely impressive, and if the UCA had left a single, physical representation of all it had achieved, the sight of the Moon covering the Sun 'exactly' at the time of a solar eclipse must surely be the first and most tangible signal to our species to 'look and understand'. Solar eclipses as seen from Earth have been described, even by unimaginative scientists, as being 'beyond incredible' and nothing of the like occurs anywhere else in the solar system.

So, there are weirdly repeating ratio-based values concerning the size of the Earth, Moon, and Sun, and relating to the orbit of the Moon around the Earth, but what about the Earth's rotation around the Sun?

The Earth completes one orbit of the Sun once every 366 days (from an Earth-bound perspective it appears to us that there are 365 days to an Earth year because we take note of sunrises. However, the motion around the Sun over the year is actually 366 rotations). The really strange thing is that the number 366 is repeated time and again just as is the ubiquitous 27.322. Just as one example, in terms of its size the Earth is 366% larger than the Moon. Therefore there is a double whammy concerning the orbital periods of our planet and its moon, measured in current Earth days. The Moon takes the same number of days to pass once around the Earth as its percentage size to Earth, and Earth takes the same number of days to pass once around the Sun as its percentage size to the Moon.

Put simply it can be observed that in terms of absolute relative sizes: the Earth x the Moon = 1. This is true to an astonishing accuracy of 5 decimal places (3.66 x 0.27322). Check it out.

Mind-boggling stuff! But what about relative mass? Surely the UCA could not have also managed to include its messages with this regard too?

The Moon is strangely light for such a large physical body, and has a mass that is 81 times less than that of the relatively heavier Earth. This value of 81 seems like another arbitrary number, but again, it is a particularly interesting number because it is a rather conspicuous 3 to the power of 4, meaning that it is 3 x 3 x 3 x 3. Is this also a part of the intended message?

But what about the little interloper left so conspicuously in the asteroid belt — the strange little world humanity chose to call Ceres? Could that tiny planet hold anything of interest?

At this point the reader might not be entirely surprised to learn that Ceres is 27.322% smaller than the Moon. What is more its mass is 81 times less than the Moon (3 to the power of 4). (Just to make this absolutely plain, the Moon is 3.66 times smaller than the Earth and has only 1/81st part of the mass of the Earth, and Ceres is 3.66 times smaller than the Moon and has only 1/81st part of the mass of the Moon.) This is incredible, and to all intents and purposes impossible — but it is so. There can surely be no doubt that in its creation of tiny Ceres the UCA was deliberately drawing attention to the

Earth/Moon relationship by leaving a 'Sentinel' that could not be overlooked, in other words something that could be termed a 'set and forget' beacon.

It is also worth noting that Ceres was manufactured in such a way that from a distance it actually 'looks' like Earth's Moon. Any view of it through a telescope or even from a spacecraft shows it to be pristine and bright in magnitude, which has been achieved in an ingenious way. Because of the nature of the composition of Ceres, anything that falls on its surface is quite quickly subsumed into the body of the little planet. Had this not been the case and after four billion years Ceres would have looked like a dusty and pockmarked nonentity — not so different in looks from any of its asteroid companions. As it is, Ceres appears to be quite different than anything around it and it does, from a distance at least, look like Earth's Moon.

The Moon left and Ceres right

We have a situation here that is like Russian dolls — one inside another yet perfectly alike. The UCA went to great lengths to ensure that Ceres would point in no uncertain terms to the fact that an entire planet had been destroyed in order to create our life support machine.

This reoccurring Russian doll relationship of Earth–Moon and Moon–Ceres is beyond any possible coincidence.

In causing all of these randomly impossible repeated numbers to fall out of the solar system objects in question, the UCA made absolutely clear what it had done. Starting with the fixed fact of the circumference of the Sun the UCA rebuilt the Earth, constructed the Moon, and identified the planet it had broken apart to provide the raw materials it needed. This is a message of supreme elegance that goes yet one more brilliant step further to 'hallmark' a deliberate and impossible to ignore communication to us humans. To move the argument on it is worth us considering what might have happened if a very simple version of this message had come to us by way of radio signals of the sort with which SETI is obsessed, rather than observing it built into the nature of solar system bodies.

A Gold Standard Communication

Imagine for a moment that SETI's scanning of the heavens has just come across two sets of repeated pulses which go on for days or weeks; 54,289 pulses and then 732 pulses. The precise repetition appears to indicate an intelligent source rather than some kind of natural occurrence. Then one of the team realises that the first number has a neat square root of 233. Naturally, those observing immediately spot that 233 is an interesting number which, amongst other things, is a Fibonacci prime number. The SETI operatives are mesmerised — and they then consider the second, shorter part of the message, which is made up of 732 pulses — and which does not have an integer square root.

They quickly deduce something of great significance: 732 divided by 233 is 3.1416, which is pi expressed to four digital places.

Wow. The SETI team would have grounds for huge excitement because the message would have spelled out the value of pi to as high a level of accuracy as is possible for an irrational number turned into a short digital pulse. This realisation would set bells ringing all over the world. The champagne would flow, and the

President of the US would give a speech from the Oval Office of the White House because we would suddenly know that we are not alone. The chances of this message being a natural signal from some object in space would be zero, and the attention of astronomers all over the planet would be focused on the radio frequency in question.

Those now locked into the signals might then wonder why the originators of the message chose to transmit the number 54,289 rather than going straight to 233? There must be a reason for using the squared value — and the answer would be that the agency transmitting the signals is asking us to draw a diagram, which could only be that of a circle sitting inside a square.

The 54,289 gives a square with sides of 233 units, which means that a circle inside that square will have a circumference of 732 units — which is the same as the second pulsed value.

Here SETI would see an intergalactic proof of pi. The hypothetical radio message from aliens does not exist but it has been built into the dimensions of the Earth, Moon, and Ceres. A square around the circle of the Earth's circumference is the length of the Earth + Moon, and a square around the Moon is equal to the Moon + Ceres. This gives pi to four decimal places — 3.1416.

Of course no such radio signal has been received by SETI — but it has been without any shadow of a doubt included in the message built into the Earth, Moon, and Ceres!

This image of a circle inside a square is effectively the logo or badge to represent the UCA that gave us life. This because to an accuracy of 99.99%, when the circle represents the circumference of the Earth, the four sides of the square are equal to the length of the circumference of the Earth plus the length of the circumference of the Moon. This is because it is a fundamental truth of geometry that the length of any square is always 27.324% longer than the circumference of the circle that fits to the sides inside it. The Moon and the Earth are massive rocky, near spherical objects that, as best we can measure, were created or altered in such a way that the length of the circumference of both added together is 27.322% longer than that of the Earth alone. Therefore to an accuracy better than 99.99% the same ratio applies — in engineering terms this is simply staggering accuracy! Our planet and its moon are the embodiment of this diagram of the two most fundamental shapes in the universe. And that level of accuracy is truly the 'gold standard' because 24 karat or pure gold is actually 99.99% pure. There is no higher form of gold other than 24k, and there is no finer definition of the relationship of our Moon and our home planet than the majestic symbol of the circle inside the square.

Of course the same relationship was applied to the relative dimensions of the Moon and Ceres.

This stunning message, with all of its repeating values, was laid down nearly 4,000,000,000 years ago — with the clear intention of us, the ultimate intelligent life form, recognising what was done for is.

There must be a very good reason why we need to know.

Chapter Nine

Drone Engineering

As we have pointed out, there simply are no candidate theories of how life originated on Earth — other than that of 'directed panspermia'. Scientific research shows conclusively that the first entities that are classified as 'life' were massively complex bacteria that sprang into existence coded by their own DNA. As we have seen, many leading thinkers have pointed this out, yet schools and even some universities across the planet still talk about life miraculously assembling itself around lightning strikes hitting a brew of swirling chemicals — the perpetuation of what has been called a 'failed paradigm'.

From leading astronomers like Sir Fred Hoyle through to brilliant atheist philosophers such as Antony Flew, the obvious conclusion has been drawn that life on our planet must have been a deliberate act. Since for the moment the identity of the intelligence that planted life here some 3.5 billion years ago is unknown, we have labelled it as the Unknown Creative Agency (UCA).

The obvious first thought is that the UCA was an advanced civilization of aliens from elsewhere in our galaxy or even beyond. Whoever or whatever the UCA was, or still is, it had no intention that we should remain ignorant as to its actions and went to great trouble to ensure that we would understand what has been done to produce intelligent life on Earth. It informed us of its presence by means of repeated mathematical patterns that draw our attention to every aspect of its grand plan.

The UCA clearly understood the vast period of time that would need to elapse between the initial seeding of life and the end point of a living planet with creatures that had begun to travel in space and were able to carefully measure the solar system and the vast reaches of space. In order to achieve its objective the UCA needed to either make its message to us exquisitely small or astronomically large, ensuring in this way that it would endure the billions of years involved.

In fact the UCA did both!

In addition to the careful ratio patterns that the UCA built into three solar system objects it also designed DNA and structured viruses to interact with living bacteria, such that it would make a journey across countless eons to eventually produce a mobile, dexterous, self-aware creature capable of abstract thought.

There were some monumental challenges in both the minuscule and massive levels. The UCA had to remodel the Earth with great exactitude, and build the Moon and Ceres from scratch, ensuring that their size, mass, and movement would be just right to bear the necessary message. In the case of DNA, it appears that this was programmed to cause major watershed events; most especially the Great Oxidation Revolution, when early forms of life had to produce the very oxygen that would wipe out most of what had gone before, and by so doing enable a whole new order of oxygen breathers to flourish. Much more recently other key events paved the way for the eventual arrival of our own species, with plants appearing across the barren earth, creating land rich in food that paved the way for vertebrate fish to crawl out of the oceans. Later there was the transition from egg layers to mammals, and eventually the apes that found they could prosper better away from the trees and by walking the savannah on two legs. And of course, because of the oxygen in the atmosphere — the same oxygen upon which they depended for their lives — these first 'thinking apes' learned to master fire.

Then followed the advent of hunter-gatherers with their wooden and flint tools durable enough to take down even large animals to skin and cook. And finally it was as recently as 10,000 years ago that some tribal groups worked out that it would be more efficient to corral animals for milk, shearing, eating, and using their hides as leather or fur. This intellectual leap led our hominid ancestors to gather plant seeds and clear ground for farming.

Given that it is believed that humans have not changed significantly in terms of brain power for around a hundred thousand years, it is strange that it took our species so long to reason out the benefits of farming over living literally hand-to-mouth, searching for prey and plants on a daily basis. It almost feels that something triggered a dramatic mental change at a specific point in time. This is reminiscent of Arthur C. Clarke's movie treatment in *2001: A Space Odyssey*, in which a particular hominid apparently has its brain remapped by the alien black monolith, which enables the species to eventually develop from the use of simple bone tools right through to the creation of spacecraft.

Could it be that this strangely recent transition from hunter-gatherer to agriculture was due to programming within human DNA, or perhaps was it another case of a virus causing a phase-change in reasoning powers?

It seems certain that DNA arrived on Earth already containing the instructions for development; and that viruses were, from the start, part of a double act — remodelling the DNA like micro engineers. We were fascinated by the power of viruses and our research showed that recent discoveries have created a great deal of curiosity about the nature of these highly sophisticated supposedly 'dead' entities.

An international team of scientists has discovered there is a huge volume of viruses circling above the planet's weather systems but below the level of airline travel. Very little is known about this realm but a team working in the Sierra Nevada mountains in Spain has calculated that some 800 million viruses cascade onto every square metre of the planet each day.

A number of researchers have stated that they believe these viruses come from outer space as a result of panspermia. In 2017, three experts called for a new initiative to better understand viral ecology, especially as the planet changes. Matthew B.

Sullivan of Ohio State University, Joshua Weitz of Georgia Tech, and Steven W. Wilhelm of the University of Tennessee wrote: "Viruses modulate the function and evolution of all living things ... but to what extent remains a mystery."

A virus injects its own DNA into the host, and these new genes are sometimes useful to the host and become part of its genome. Researchers recently identified an ancient virus that inserted its DNA into the genomes of four-limbed animals that were our ancestors. This tiny piece of genetic code, designated as ARC, is now part of the nervous system of modern humans and has an important role in our consciousness, including nerve communication, memory formation, and higher-order thinking. Scientists estimate that between 40% and 80% of our current human genome is directly linked to countless viral invasions over many millions of years.

Not only are viruses responsible for directing the evolution of all species on Earth including ourselves; they have also been identified as very precise controllers of our global environment. This was demonstrated in laboratory experiments where viruses were filtered out of seawater leaving only bacteria — the host that is normally invaded by the viruses. The researchers found that without viruses the plankton in the water immediately stop growing, because nutrients such as nitrogen were no longer liberated. This is hugely important as when plankton grows, it takes in carbon dioxide and excretes oxygen. One study estimated that viruses in our seas cause a trillion, trillion infections every second thereby destroying one-fifth of all bacterial cells in the sea every single day! This shows how viruses help keep the world's ecosystem balanced by changing the composition of microbial communities, so that if, for example, a toxic algae bloom spreads in the ocean, it is controlled by a virus attack, which causes it to explode and die very rapidly.

The bottom line is that everything alive on our planet is here because of viruses, which are highly complex entities that are themselves stone dead. Without viruses life would never have started or progressed, and if they ceased to exist we would almost certainly quickly disappear.

The existence of such wonderful microscopic engineers surely cannot be dismissed as a happy accident. It is considered to be normal and reasonable simply to accept that they are present because of some unknowable mechanism, which seems to us to be unlikely and unreasonable. Viruses like bacteria are super-complex machines that don't come into existence by random happenstance — and the way they work together to evolve species and keep our ecosystem in fine balance is nothing less than totally miraculous.

Any rational person (like Professors Flew and Hoyle) has to accept that we are looking at a planned mechanism rather than idly ignoring the wall of evidence simply because some establishment figures are reticent to acknowledge that conscious planning was behind life on Earth. Whether this is due to the presence of some sort of deity or an intergalactic federation of super-beings, we have to confront an inescapable truth.

Once science officially accepts the obvious and puts away the deeply flawed notion of the over simple model proposed by Darwinian evolution, with its random mutations linked to 'survival of the fittest', serious research can be funded to look closely at the causation of major changes that led to our current 'advanced' status. As we have seen, we now know how a virus reprogramed reptiles to create mammals, but what caused our ancestors to walk on two legs? And how did our forebears develop a voice box that was essential in beginning the process of developing language?

This last example is worth a closer look because humanity could never have progressed in the way it did without language. When researchers examined the voice box (the larynx), in 43 different species of primates they found that humans differ from apes and monkeys because humans lack a small structure called a vocal membrane and balloon-like structures called air sacs that allow other primates to produce loud, deep calls. The loss of these tissues resulted in a stable vocal system in humans that was critical to the development of human speech, which in turn permits humans to express sophisticated thoughts and feelings using clear and highly defined sounds.

The loss of these small anatomical features cleared the way for the development of speech that would eventually lead to writing and indeed eventually to mathematics. When this happened is debated but is usually considered to have been around as recently as 70,000 to 200,000 years ago. It is now thought that our near relative, the Neanderthals, which disappeared around 40,000 years ago, had speech as sophisticated as Homo sapiens.

Given that we have no option but to acknowledge that human existence was carried out to a plan and that viruses are the primary tool to engineer rapid change, it seems that the UCA is somehow aware of our progress and 'firing' in viruses to carry out the work. Because the gigantic virus cloud is high up in our atmosphere, above the weather, it is not slowed by friction with the planet's surface and distribution to every continent is almost instantaneous.

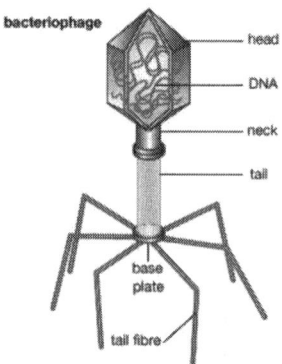

The bacteriophage (bacterial virus) shown here has a head shaped like an icosahedron (with 20 sides). The tail fibres attach the virus to the bacterium, bringing the base plate into contact with the surface. The tail contracts, and DNA from the head is injected into the host.

The virus bacteriophage T4, from the family Myoviridae, is described by experts as an intriguing contractile injection machine to inject its genome into its target, but the dynamics of its injection machinery remain unknown. Simulations of the invasion by the virus conducted by a team led by Ameneh Maghsoodi from the Department of Mechanical Engineering, University of Michigan, have described the dynamical pathway of the injection process as a "contraction wave" that propagates along the sheath. They report how the energy that powers the injection machinery also drives the forces responsible for piercing the host cell membrane, and the controls of the timescale of the injection process.

For what most biologists consider a non-living natural object, a virus is extremely strange and is clearly designed to carry out a precise function. It looks more like a space landing craft and it behaves like an automated hypodermic drone to target and inject its own DNA into its target. As viruses are not alive they can have no motivation to multiply or ability to seek benefit — so it appears they could be acting on behalf of another intelligent entity. Calling this entity a drone seems to be entirely apposite as it is an inanimate object carrying out a task for someone, or something else — which we would suggest is the UCA.

Chapter Ten

So Who Was It That Built the Earth?

No matter who or what the Unknown Creative Agency might be. It seems appropriate first to discount the idea of a deity representing the UCA since a truly omnipotent being would have simply willed the Earth and Moon to come into existence in its finished form rather than engineer it bit by bit. It might be reasonable perhaps to argue that the whole universe and its infrastructure, that appeared so instantaneously at the moment of the 'Big Bang', based on mathematics and the laws of physics, were down to an all powerful deity, but the building of our planet and its seeding with DNA was most certainly a local event.

If we put aside the God option, that leaves just two possibilities that occur to us; the UCA either represents an intervention by aliens from another part of our Galaxy or beyond, or it was humans from our own future, who travelled backwards in time to undertake the massive adventure in engineering and to initiate life on Earth.

The idea that there was an amazingly advanced alien species in existence 4.5 billion years ago is plausible, as there has been around three times that length of time since the start of the universe, and before the building of our planet and its moon. However, according to a recent discovery, the universe is twice as old as previously thought, at 27 billion years. This startling revelation came from evidence gathered by the famous James Webb Space Telescope, which is observing the universe at an unprecedented super-resolution. This amazingly powerful instrument has examined the cosmic background radiation, the most distant galaxies, and the oldest known stars. The data collected has been analysed by a team of world-renowned scientists and has provided the definitive answer to the question of how many years have elapsed since the Big Bang. This means that the universe is six times older than our solar system.

And it seems that that was not the beginning anyway. Leading lights such as Sir Roger Penrose, who is regarded as one of the greatest living physicists, mathematicians and scientists, are categorical that the Big Bang did happen, but that it was not the starting point of creation.

However old the cosmos is, there could indeed be entities that spend the eons seeding new life wherever they find suitable candidate planets orbiting stars like our Sun. These hypothetical aliens would presumably be motivated by the desire to sow and grow intelligent life across the entire cosmos — for surely our little corner of space is too insignificant for our world to be a one-off from their theoretical perspective.

However, the invention of this entirely hypothetical super-advanced alien culture does bring a major problem: Where is that super culture now, because if it was capable of such a feat of Astro-engineering all of those billions of years ago, it would surely have achieved a totally godlike level of ultimate power by this era? If this was the case, such a culture would have achieved a stage at which it could do anything instantly — and anywhere. The whole situation strikes us as being fundamentally unlikely.

Whilst all the busy operatives at SETI are spending many millions of dollars every year seeking a message from an assumed intelligence beyond our Earth, there is not a shred of proof that such a thing even exists. The whole notion of creatures from another planet appears to be driven by humanity's desire not to be alone in this vast cosmos. However, if we apply the principle of Occam's Razor to what has taken place in our own corner of the universe, there is no requirement to invent aliens at all.

There is a rather useful thought experiment concerning a murder in a sealed bank vault that illustrates the point we are making. Two men enter the vault for a period of 24 hours and guards stand watch at the door. When the door is unlocked the guards find that one of the infiltrators is dead, having been stabbed through the heart. Investigators confirm that there is no weapon in the room and no other way in or out other than through the safe door, which had remained locked for the duration. How was this killing conducted in the absence of a dagger, and who could the murderer be? After considering a number of weird ideas, including the possibility of an alien beaming itself through the atomic structure of the steel walls, those responsible arrest the second man who had spent the day in the vault. He maintains that he is innocent, pointing out that he does not possess a weapon and therefore could not have committed the attack. However, after a great deal of thought, a particularly bright police investigator eventually reasons that the second man had brought a deeply frozen icicle into the vault, concealed inside his night bag, which he had quickly plunged into the chest of his companion, killing him before the ice melted and the remaining water merged with the blood of the dying victim.

This story illustrates the point that, as in the case of the bank vault, an outside agency does not have to be invoked and there is only one conceivable culprit present for the terraforming of the Earth and the manufacture of the Moon. Humanity itself must have been responsible. All that remains is to work out how this could have been possible.

So, when it comes to identifying the UCA; and if we are 'really' to apply Occam's razor there is only one known creature in the entire universe of which we are aware that would be capable of building the Earth and the Moon and that is us — for does not the history of humanity prove conclusively that up until this point in time 'if we can think it, sooner or later we will achieve it'? Of course we are not yet clever enough to conduct such a feat, but if we continue to progress, presumably one day we will be. We also have the DNA already to hand with which to start life, so 'all' we need to do is to go back a few billion years to begin the process.

But such a thing cannot be possible. Can it?

Time and Tide

Walt Disney is reputed to have said, "If you can dream something you can do it," and in the case of human beings this so often seems to be true. As a species we are so clever and innovative that what we think of today frequently turns out to be tomorrow's reality.

As an example, there was a seminal television series that became the launch pad for so much that followed in terms of science fiction. It was in the year 1966 that *Star Trek* first appeared on our screens. The series dealt with a starship called the *Enterprise*, the crew of which travelled through the galaxy and became involved in adventures that although looking 'creaky' by the standards of today's film and television with its CGI and lavish settings, nevertheless enthralled viewers at the time.

One of the objects that appeared regularly in that first *Star Trek* series and which captivated viewers was the 'communicator', a hand-held device with which members of the *Enterprise* crew kept in touch with their ship and with each other. These communicators were about the size of a modern mobile phone and had flip tops, which when opened immediately caused the device to make contact with the *Enterprise* or other crew members. Paradoxically, although *Star Trek* was set in the 23rd century, the mythical communicators used in the series were extremely primitive in comparison with their modern counterparts. They dealt in sound only, had no view screen and were extremely limited in their capabilities. Nevertheless, these devices seemed quite amazing at the time.

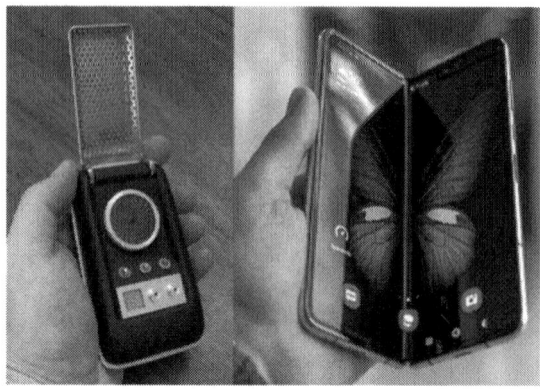

A '23rd century' Star Trek *communicator and a modern folding phone.*
Notice the three coloured buttons have changed from physical three-dimensional
lumps to touch sensitive, virtual ones.

A fairly primitive mobile phone, an advanced, hand-held version of which almost everyone on our planet now possesses, did not appear until 1983 — long after *Star Trek* had commenced, so there was no comparison at the time.

How things have changed — and how quickly. Each of our present day smartphones can be connected to over thirty communication satellites in Earth orbit and can direct us to almost any location on the surface of our planet; mobile phones not only keep us in touch with each other face to face, they allow us to communicate with our banks, carrying out endless transactions on line and in shops, they can answer almost any question we wish to ask, and are able to connect us immediately to the greatest reservoir of knowledge that has ever existed. Our smartphones take professional class photographs and movies, and can help to keep us physically fit whilst monitoring all our bodily functions; they allow us to be allied to all manner of social and professional platforms, and of course they alert us to news and world happenings in a moment-by-moment sense. How far removed they are from our conception of such a device only a few decades ago.

What is extremely interesting is that the memories within our smartphones are controlled by quantum mechanics, in which electrons do not exist at a specific point but are held in a probability cloud outside of time and space. This allows them to move between physical walls inside the memory cell to provide a record of data.

So much else we now take for granted has appeared in an almost frighteningly short period of time. Devices such as microwave ovens were not even thought of until the end of the Second World War, and electric cars, though conceived at the beginning of the 20th century, did not become a viable reality until incredibly recently. Meanwhile computers, which only appeared after 1945, have doubled in power every two years since the 1970s, and Artificial Intelligence (AI) with all its incredible implications is now a reality. In this area alone the power and versatility of computers has been staggering. Our modern computers are so advanced and have improved at such a rate that it is often pointed out that the memory capacity of the computers used to send the first astronauts to the Moon was 250,000 times less powerful than a typical laptop today; and about the same as that available to a modern and very modest calculator.

We have to remember that it was not until 1961 that the first human being left the surface of our planet to travel (albeit for an incredibly short period of time) in space. Within the lifetime of individuals alive today humanity has advanced further in terms of technology than was the case in all the previous centuries we have been on this planet. With the pace of technology stepping up all the time it does not take much of an imagination to realise that what stands before us will be breathtaking in its scope and consequences. Whatever mistakes we might have made on the way, nobody could deny that human beings are remarkable creatures and nor could they doubt that what might seem impossible or incredible at this moment is likely to become the norm in a very short period. This, we dare to believe, will include the ability to manipulate time itself.

The concept of time travel first appeared in an ancient manuscript known as the Mahabharata from India in around 400 BC, though in a modern sense it was first dealt with by the author HG Wells in his book *The Time Machine*, which was published in 1895. The hero of Wells' book moved easily back and forth through time in a contraption he had built himself. The book was an instant success, and the intriguing notion of being able to visit periods from the past or future has been of tremendous popularity in literature, on television, and in movies ever since. The concept of time travel appears so regularly in entertainment that especially to many members of the younger generation, it is almost a 'given'. Its reality would undoubtedly surprise us but we have been well conditioned to accept it.

In the early days of the 20th century most scientists would have viewed the work of HG Wells as being pure fantasy. That was until a physicist by the name of Igor Novikov came along and brought with him the mathematics that showed time travel to be feasible.

Up until the time of Novikov, who put forward his seminal work in the mid-1980s, travelling in time seemed to be a philosophical impossibility, quite aside from the practical difficulties it would present. The scepticism stemmed from potential problems concerning the paradoxical nature of time travel, and especially so to the past. These problems were summed up in a story known as the 'Grandfather Paradox', which is still trotted out by those who imagine the whole notion of travelling in time is absurd.

The story suggests that someone with a vendetta against his or her own grandfather might choose to go back in time in order to shoot him as a young man. Of course, the critics comment, this could not be possible for a very simple reason. If one's grandfather was killed earlier in time than the birth of the protagonist's father (or mother), the person in question could never have been born. Admittedly this is an extreme example but it does seem to point to an apparent problem when it comes to travelling into the past.

Russian-born physicist Igor Novikov was aware of the Grandfather Paradox, but he was more interested in the physics of the situation. He spent a great deal of time working on the problem and eventually came up with what is known as the 'principle of self-consistency', which would allow for travel into the past within the realms of what is understood about physics today; but only under very specific circumstances. Novikov agreed that to make any changes to a past that had already happened would not be possible, but with regard to the physics and mathematics involved, there was still no obstacle to such a journey taking place. In the view of Igor Novikov, and all other mainstream physicists today, although it would not be possible to go back in time to kill one's own grandfather, it would be feasible to travel to the grandfather's period in time and, for example, 'prevent' him from being killed — perhaps by representing a mysterious stranger who pulled him out of the path of a speeding vehicle. Such a happening would already be written into the framework of history and so would not break the natural rules applicable to the flow of time. We can see from this example that an incursion into the past (from a philosophical view) would not only be possible but might have a real and observable effect. However, it need not appear to be particularly extraordinary on the part of those present, and viewed from a future perspective it would become nothing more than just another part of the timeline from the period in question.

Since incursions into the past (according to Novikov and borne out by the laws of physics) cannot alter anything that 'must' become part of the future's history, if they exist at all, they could only do so to 'confirm' events and not to 'contradict' them.

If we look carefully at human history, it is possible to see specific events that could so easily have represented an incursion from the future. We cite one example below which although it cannot be proven to have been a temporal incursion has all the hallmarks of such a happening. Like many other possible examples it does not contradict Novikov's principle of self-consistency and so we stress there is nothing in the realm of physics to say it could not have taken place. We cite this potential example simply to show that not only could one travel to the past but that an interaction with that past would be possible — and in fact might be essential.

On Tuesday September 11th, 2001, the United States suffered a day that would shake the nation to its core. It was on this day that the Twin Towers of the World Trade Center in New York were destroyed by a pair of commercial aircraft used as missiles, and the Pentagon in Washington DC was badly damaged by another aircraft. At the control of these planes were terrorists and the result of their efforts saw over 2900 people dead and a world that would be altered forever.

The story is well known but there are certain aspects of what took place that although significant are not really talked about much, since they seem to be self-evident. We refer specifically to what took place at the Pentagon on that terrible day.

The Pentagon is the headquarters of the United States Military. It is a massive building which stands close to Washington DC and is, as its name suggests, a five-sided structure. Only someone who, like us, has stood next to the Pentagon can begin to understand its huge dimensions. On the fateful day it housed around 18,000 workers, and because of its association with the military aspect of the United States, it presented a prime target for the terrorists on 9/11.

At 9.27 on that terrible morning American Airlines Flight 77 slammed into the western face of the Pentagon. The aircraft continued well into the outer ring of the building causing severe fires that took days to extinguish, and the floors above the impact collapsed, forming a heap of debris that hindered the rescue personnel from retrieving the injured and dead. When a count could finally be made it was discovered that 125 people had died and there were many injuries. The impact upon the family and friends of those who died on that morning is incalculable but the amazing fact associated with the disaster is that so few people lost their lives at the Pentagon, and for a very important reason.

Prior to 1998, three years before 9/11, it had been decided that the entire Pentagon should be strengthened, chiefly because the building had been thrown up just as the United States was entering the Second World War and it had been decided that use of iron or steel in the structure should be kept to a minimum, since such metals were crucial to war efforts. As a result, concrete had been the material of choice, which was fine for normal purposes but not for a building that might one day be attacked — as indeed proved to be the case. This had not been an issue during World War II because at that time no enemy could reach that part of the United States, though approaching the end of the century the Pentagon was overdue for modernisation and strengthening. In 1998, work on the Pentagon began and the first side of the building that was chosen was the west side.

New windows were fitted that carried very modern blast-resistant glass, and the structure of the building's face on the western side was also massively strengthened. This extensive work had only been completed days prior to the 9/11 attack, and as a result there were virtually no people working in the western part of the building on that day since most of those who normally worked there had been moved to different parts of the Pentagon or to other buildings entirely.

A conservative estimate after the event suggested that the death toll from the 9/11 attack on the Pentagon, if the western side of the building had not been strengthened, could easily have exceeded 2000. Beyond this estimation some engineers have suggested that the aircraft, loaded as it was with fuel and hitting the building at a speed in excess of 350 miles per hour, could have broken through the outer ring of the building and continued through to the very centre of the Pentagon, in which case many more people could have died — perhaps five or six thousand. This means that at the very least a possible 1800 or many more people survived 9/11 because the western side of the building had been strengthened.

The possibility of the terrorists at the controls of Flight 77 choosing to fly into the western face of the Pentagon were 1 in 5, and it is feasible that the whole situation was simply one of chance, in which case those in the building merely got lucky. On the other hand if it was possible for someone to travel from the future and to influence the order in which the strengthening of the Pentagon took place and the dates upon which the work was undertaken it would also have been possible to affect the outcome of the 9/11 attack in that location — without in any way changing the established timeline or altering events as we read of them in our history books today.

The likely path of Flight 77 as it hit the western side of the Pentagon on 9/11 if the face of the structure on that side had not been significantly strengthened. The plane loaded with fuel could well have extended through all five rings of the building, resulting in thousands of deaths.

There is no doubt that there are still some scientists in the world who would prefer that for some unknown reason time travel must be deemed impossible, but the simple truth is that the possibility has not been disproved and is held as being tenable in terms of what we know about the universe and the forces that govern it. The famous Cambridge physicist Stephen Hawking was alarmed by the idea of time travel, yet he knew there was no issue of science that forbad it. He speculated that maybe there was some kind of 'time police' who would simply stop it happening even though it was technically possible. On June 28th, 2009, Professor Hawking sat alone in a large room at the University of Cambridge where he was throwing a party and waited patiently for party guests to arrive. He had posted an open invitation for people from the future to join him — but not one of them showed up. This he argued was an indication that it was not possible for people from next year, the next century, or beyond to join him. But the simple answer is that people in his future knew that no one had taken up the invitation, so didn't go.

Despite Hawking's discomfort with the concept he knew full well that, despite the ultra physics language used, there is a mathematical construct known as a tachyon, which is created on a 'now' hypersurface of simultaneity that then propagates towards an 'earlier' hypersurface of simultaneity. It arrives at the earlier hypersurface that collects events from an earlier time before it was created. This means that the tachyon in question is most certainly travelling backwards in time.

Bearing in mind the work of Igor Novikov and allowing for the limitations that physics seems to place upon the 'nature' of travelling to the past, time travel remains an eventual certainty if only we can master the technical difficulties involved. Humanity being what it is, and allowing for the rise of the artificial intelligence we are already creating, which will eventually lead us to answers we have not so far dreamed of, time travel will happen. And because time travel backwards will happen in our future, there must have been visitations to our past and present.

Maybe it will be a one-way trip. This means that matter can be sent back in time but cannot return to its starting point because, if it did, instantaneously it would seem that it had never have left, according to any observer.

Working out 'how' we could travel in time leads us in the present era to the world of speculation. A whole book could be filled with the various theories that already exist, but to get to the heart of the matter, travelling in time is going to take a great deal of power and probably the ability to harness antimatter, and that most incredible and to most people barely perceptible subject of quantum physics. Idle speculation is probably somewhat pointless at this stage of our understanding but the existence of situations such as the one that took place at the Pentagon on the day of 9/11, together with other occurrences from the past that have all the hallmarks of time incursions from the future, seem to point to the inevitability of something that writers and scientific speculators since the time of HG Wells have accepted as being inevitable. We would suggest that without the reality of time travel our world could not exist as it is today.

The Dinosaur Paradox

There is another pointer to our existence being due to humans from the future rather than an assumed extraterrestrial intelligence, and that is the existence of the rise and fall of the dinosaurs. These often huge egg layers ruled the Earth for around 185 million years until they suddenly disappeared 66 million years ago, leaving the way open for what had been small shrew-like creatures to develop into the range of mammals we see today, including ourselves.

If aliens had been responsible for building our planet as an incubator and seeding it with programmed DNA, they would have focused on something more like a straight line from bacteria through to ourselves. There would have been no need to build in the cul-de-sac of history that was the dinosaurs. However, if the UCA are humans from our own future they would have had to go along with this age of giant lizards because that is what happened. They simply could not change it even if they wanted to.

For some people reading this book, there will be puzzlement and possibly denial. 'How can people from the future be responsible for making the past?' It can seem like a circular argument; and so it is. But there are no rules against circles in time according to the laws of physics. To say that the whole idea is counter-intuitive is entirely correct, but that is the nature of quantum mechanics — of which time travel will no doubt be a part. In the quantum world things are known to happen that defy any normal logic or reasoning — including particles that have to rotate twice through 360 degrees to return to their original position and individual electrons that are in several different locations at the same time!

It really seems that the answer is right in front of us. Just as it says in the beginning of the Christian bible, in Genesis 1:26: "Let us make man in our image, after our likeness".

A Calling Card

Having identified that travelling in time is the answer to our quest, we wondered whether the people from our future had left a message to confirm their role. And we believe that they have done.

In Chapter 8 we pointed out that there is a reoccurring number when the mass of the Moon is compared to that of the Earth, and of Ceres compared to the Moon. In both instances it is a factor of 81, which is 3 to the power of 4 ($3 \times 3 \times 3 \times 3$). This appears to be a great big finger pointing towards time travel. The 3 can be taken as a reference to normal Euclidean space (height, width, and depth), which dictates a cube and the power of four is pointing to the time element — a fourth dimension. There is something called 'Minkowski spacetime', which is a concept that shows how a spacetime interval between any two events is independent of the inertial frame of reference in which they are recorded. Minkowski space is closely associated with Einstein's theories of special relativity and general relativity, and is the most common mathematical structure by which special relativity is formalised. While the individual components in Euclidean space and time might differ due to length contraction and time dilation, in Minkowski spacetime, all frames of reference will agree on the total interval in spacetime between events. Minkowski space differs from four-dimensional Euclidean space insofar as it treats time differently than the three spatial dimensions.

There is also a geometric object called a tesseract, which is the four-dimensional analogue of the cube; the tesseract is to the cube as the cube is to the square. Just as the surface of the cube consists of six square faces, the hypersurface of the tesseract consists of eight cubical cells. The tesseract is one of the six convex regular 4-polytopes.

Chapter Eleven

Units Matter

Having spent the best part of a quarter of a century agonising over the identity of the UCA that caused life to exist on Earth, we have finally decided that it was almost certainly our own offspring from the future. There is simply far more logic to this conclusion than any other, including any supposed alien civilization.

The realisation caused us to revisit a topic that has puzzled us all the way through our long journey of research. This is the curious fact that the number patterns that have been built into our part of the solar system include many examples that only exist when viewed in human-defined units of measurement. It is one thing to identify 'dimensionless relationships', which exist outside of any particular convention, but quite another when what we are looking at are cultural creations.

Unitless numbers are real values that exist independently of culture. Pi for example represents the ratio of a circle's circumference to its diameter and has no units. It is not 3.1416 metres or 3.1416 yards or even 3.1416 hat stands. The definition of pi will always be defined as 3.1416, no matter where and how it appears. So when unrelated ratio numbers turn up that display repeating perfect integers in base-ten, these particular numbers stand out. An example of this is the Moon being 400 times smaller than the Sun but 400 times closer to the surface of the Earth than to the Sun. As we have pointed out, this remarkable reality means that a person standing on the surface of the Earth sees the disc of the Moon perfectly eclipse the disc of the Sun on occasions when they overlap in the daytime sky. And there are other ratio based oddities such as the speed of Earth's orbit around the Sun being a very neat one-ten-thousandth part of the speed of light.

We have already outlined the list of repeating and interrelated values that are so conspicuous in terms of the Earth and the Sun; values that would be recognised by high intelligence anywhere across our galaxy or beyond, but over the last quarter of a century we have also puzzled over the existence of conspicuous numerical values in the solar system that are reliant on units that are cultural creations and therefore would be meaningless for any external observer. We have commented that these exist, but have not focused on them because they could have been nothing more than curious accidents.

As an example, it is a strange fact that the Moon rotates on its axis at an astonishingly neat one hundredth of the rate of the turn of the Earth on its axis. This is extremely curious in itself but when the modern metric system is applied to the distances involved — the situation goes crazy! The Earth turns through 40,000 kilometres per day and the Moon turns 400 kilometres on its own axis in the same period. We were very perplexed by such a weird situation — and the same value of '400' as we had seen so often elsewhere appearing once again seemed to be pointing towards something very significant.

Despite these peculiarities it was not the presence of a regular and astonishing fit in metric units that first caught our attention — it was the perfect resonance of Stone Age units of measure that had alerted us to the fact that there is something very odd about our Moon — at least in comparison with the Earth. Back in the late 1990s, we were working on identifying the scientific origins of a system of Neolithic units discovered by the late Alexander Thom, a highly respected professor of engineering from Oxford University (after whom the mathematics faculty building was named). Thom had spent several decades surveying Megalithic structures from the late Stone Age around the British Isles and this had allowed him to demonstrate statistically that the Scottish stone circles had been used to track the Moon and would thus have been useful for assisting in the understanding of tides, information that would have been invaluable to the Megalithic sailors. He also discerned a system of metrology based around a unit of length that he named the Megalithic Yard. This basic unit was 2.722 feet (+/- 0.002 feet), which is 82.966 cm. We had been able to explain that this unit was created using a pendulum and a unique geometry based on a 366 degree circle. Our thesis on this subject was published in our book, *Civilization One*. It was checked thoroughly by expert mathematicians and found to be correct. (See Appendix 2.)

We were able to demonstrate that this Stone Age system of metrology based on a geometry that assumed 366 degrees to a circle was not restricted to the Megalithic Yard as a unit of length but extended also to weight, volume, capacity, time, and apparently even temperature (in a scale in which water freezes at zero degrees and boils at 366 degrees, absolute zero, the lowest possible temperature in such a Megalithic system of temperature would be minus 1000 degrees — precisely).

These ancient scientists divided the Earth's polar circumference into 366 Megalithic degrees, each of which were broken down into 360 seconds of arc. Each of these seconds of arc were exactly 366 Megalithic Yards in length. This represents elegance almost beyond belief, and splits the true polar circumference of the earth exactly.

We knew Professor Thom had shown that the Neolithic scientists had measured the movement of the Moon from their observatories, and had most certainly paid special attention to this object in the night sky. Meanwhile, such close attention to the Moon, whilst dealing with the Megalithic Yard, led us to notice something odd about the Moon's dimensions. Whilst the Earth is equal to 366 degrees in the Megalithic system, the Moon is equivalent to exactly 100 of the same degrees! In other words the Moon is precisely 3.66 times smaller than the Earth.

We were dumbstruck! How could people over 5000 years ago have devised a unit of length that was so fundamental to the very essence of both our planet and its moon? And by what miracle do the Earth and the Moon come to have such a beautiful dimensional relationship in any case? This was a truly significant step in our research project that would put us on the path of unravelling the nature of life on Earth.

We were understandably amazed at the existence of mathematical relationships between the Sun, Earth, Moon, and Ceres, that extended from pure ratios to units of human convention both ancient and modern. We were able to rule out a string of super-coincidences; as that would be the least plausible answer. However, it is a fact that both the Megalithic system and the metric system of measurement are both of a similar age — circa 5000 years ago.

Today the metre is defined as 'the path travelled by light in a vacuum in 1/299,792,458 part of a second'. This is interesting because the second of time has been in use since at least the third millennium BC, when it was used by the culture we call Sumerians who lived in the region around the rivers Euphrates and Tigris — modern Iraq and Kuwait. We owe a great deal to these people, including glass, writing, the wheel, and the 360 degree variety of geometry, which they knew was not accurate to the yearly calendar but it was easy to use alongside their mathematical notations. These people had units of length that they called the kush and the double-kush, the latter being the length of a pendulum that swung at a rate of once per second. This was incredibly close to what we know as a metre today, being 99.9 cm.[1] Today, people puzzle over this relationship between the metre and the second. Indeed it formed a significant part of our early research.

The Sumerians did not use a simple base ten system of numbers such as our modern convention; instead they used the numbers six and ten together to create a sexagesimal, or base 60 system. The Sumerians used this because the number 60 has no less than twelve factors, namely 1, 2, 3, 4, 5, 6, 10, 12, 15,

20, 30, and 60. With so many factors, many fractions involving sexagesimal numbers are simplified; for example one hour can be divided evenly into sections of 30 minutes, 20 minutes, 15 minutes, 12 minutes, 10 minutes, 6 minutes and 5 minutes. This system was so convenient that we still use it for the measurement of time and for geometry.

It will no doubt surprise many readers to know that the speed of light itself is pure Sumerian — and circa 5000 years old. Of course the Sumerians were not aware of the fact but the speed of light is defined as being 299,792,458 metres per second, which just happens to be an almost exact 600 million kush per second. That is a very pure sexagesimal number indeed — and as we have already seen, the second of time was a Sumerian invention in any case.

In the 18th century the French reverse-engineered the ancient metre, initially using a pendulum that swung once per second, and later they defined the metre as being 1/10,000,000th part of a quadrant of the Earth between the north pole and the equator. The French were very slightly wrong in their assessment of the Earth, which is why the polar circumference of the Earth is considered today to be a little under 40,008 kilometres.

We have long been curious as to why humankind, after such a fantastically long period of time, rather suddenly invented complex astronomy, mathematics, metal working, writing, and the wheel. It was as though someone entered a pitch-black cavern and switched on a million watt floodlight, and it so much feels like an intervention, rather similar to Arthur C. Clarke's hominid who in the movie *2001: A Space Odyssey* is trained to think about tools by the black monolith. Whilst the establishment academics just say, "Well that's just how it was, wasn't it?" — we have identified those responsible: Time-travellers from our future.

Who else could be responsible? Did the time travellers somehow put in an appearance in human form back in the fourth or fifth millennium BC to actually teach the locals, or was it achieved by a bioengineered correction to our DNA, conducted thanks to specifically designed viruses? It seems to us that the answer had to be a physical manifestation — real people who arrived and suggested to the leaders of certain groups that it would be rather useful to have universal and precise units of measurement that only required very simple tools to reproduce. To the local chiefs this would represent status and power, whilst the instructors would know that in the future these extremely sophisticated systems would stand out like a proverbial sore thumb.

It seems impossible to believe that the Stone Age inhabitants of the British Isles could have surveyed both the Earth and the Moon in order to devise a creative unit that worked for both on a deeply mathematical level, and it also seems as good as incredible that when left to their own devices these people would even have had any incentive to do so. They could, however, have been given the units and trained how to reproduce them anywhere using only wooden sticks, a few stones and lengths of rope, in conjunction with observing the rotation of the Earth as illustrated by the passage of the stars across the heavens each night. We described exactly how this was achieved in our book, *Civilization One*, and we have carried out such experiments ourselves.

Equally we can be certain that the Sumerians simply could not have had a clue about the speed of light in a vacuum. So, did strangers arrive in their midst to teach them these wonderful new ideas? Whilst the inhabitants of the British Isles did not have a system of writing to record their units or from where they originated, the Sumerians did and their history spells out very clearly exactly what happened. These teachers are referred to as the Anunnaki, 'the shining ones', or 'the watchers', and they were described as real people who were giants and white in colour. The story of these visitors passed into Hebrew tradition after the Babylonian captivity of the mid first century BC, in which the visitors are called Nephilim, a word that comes from the root word 'naphal', which means simply 'to fall', perhaps indicating a sudden arrival. It is now believed that the Jewish scholars reversed much of the ancient story cycles to take power away from the Babylonian/Mesopotamian/Sumerian originals. Working on the almost inevitable recourse we find time and again in history that one culture's God is another culture's Devil, the Jewish scholars introduced the idea that the knowledge that had been forthcoming had corrupted mankind rather than assisting it.

The story that says these people were, or gave rise to, 'giants' obviously suggests that these incomers where markedly taller than the native peoples. The average height of a Bronze Age (3rd millennium BC) Sumerian is considered to be around 165 cm (5'5") for a male and 156 cm (5'1") for a female. By comparison the average man today, in the Netherlands for example, would tower head and shoulders above a Sumerian, being over 6 feet tall.

Originally, these Anunnaki had such immense powers they were considered to be deities. In the poem *Enki and the World Order*, we are told that the Anunnaki dwell among the people of Sumer and that they "decree the fates of mankind". All advanced knowledge that did indeed suddenly appear around 5000 years ago is ascribed to these powerful strangers. We are told that one individual called Azazel taught the Sumerians how to find and work the metals of the earth, enabling them to make bracelets and ornaments — and then knives, breastplates and strong shields. Another Baraquijal explained the workings of astronomy whilst a third, Kokabiel, gave the names to the constellations. Shamsiel focused on the Sun, and Sariel the Moon. Then for farmers Semjaza gave instructions regarding agriculture such as how to take root-cuttings. Finally, meteorology was turned into a science by Ezeqeel.

Could all of this be memories of real events and might these characters have been actual time-travellers? It would be easy to dismiss such thoughts as ridiculous — if it were not for the facts that we have already outlined, which show that it is conventional explanations that are often ridiculous. Notions such as the spontaneous arrival of life on Earth as a result of chemical happenstance and the idea of the Moon resulting from a simple collision between the Earth and a Mars sized object just do not stack up. Similarly, the existence of two super-sophisticated systems of measurement that convention is willing to accept arrived simultaneously and from nowhere does not make any sense either.

It appears that the metric system was left in plain sight, but the megalithic system was allowed to disappear from view — until a superb engineer came along in the form of Alexander Thom, whose meticulous efforts and faultless recordkeeping found it again.

We were lucky enough to be the people who first noticed the detailed mathematical patterns first left in the Earth, Moon, and Ceres because we were working on discovering the origins of Alexander Thom's Megalithic Yard. The Megalithic Yard became the basis for all of the Imperial system of measurements, from pints to pounds to miles, but the principal unit, the Megalithic Yard itself, had not been used for three and a half millennia. Without this unique point of entry it would be difficult for anyone to see the enormity of the picture regarding the Earth and the Moon that was painted for us. We can only conclude that our time-travelling offspring will, some day in the near future, decide to go back some 5500 years to teach the 'sleepy' humans how to create science using measurements that matter. It appears that occasional interactions with the past were required. This was to be the key that turned in the lock. We are grateful.

End Note

[1] Knight, C. and Butler, A. *Civilization One*. Watkins, 2004.

Chapter Twelve

Why Now?

In Arthur C. Clarke and Stanley Kubrick's movie, *2001: A Space Odyssey*, the unknown entity or civilization that had elevated an unsuspecting ape to the rank of thinking human long ago had also placed a black monolith on the Moon that would trigger a signal when the descendants of this Earthly creature had advanced to the point of local space travel and exploration. This part of the plan laid down by an unknown alien presence in the movie was well thought out because the monolith placed on the Moon could not have been discovered until human beings were advanced enough to visit our neighbour in space and had also built a base there — ready to set out into the furthest reaches of the solar system.

2001: A Space Odyssey was a fascinating story and it bore some striking similarities to our own research, but what we are describing in this book is a 'real' message from a genuine agency, to tell us about what it achieved with its engineering skill in almost miraculously creating a safe home on the Earth for life to blossom. What is abundantly clear is that the UCA went to great trouble to ensure we would receive that message right now — at this precise point in the development of humanity.

Notice of the Moon's true pedigree as a manufactured object is built into every aspect of its association with the Earth and the Sun in terms of its size, mass, and orbital characteristics. However, the star of the show as far as that intended proof is concerned has to be the occurrence of total solar eclipses. These 'performances' occur thanks to the conspicuous ratios of the Moon that only come good at this particular point in the history of our planet. Had an intelligent species developed on Earth a million years before it did, or a million years after, no perfect solar eclipse would have taken place for them when viewed from the planet's surface — and the message would have missed its mark. If this was the case, the first clue left by the UCA would be unnoticed by humanity. A million years adrift might seem to be a considerable period to the average human being, but in terms of the age of the Earth it is tiny. So, it is quite obvious that the UCA knew from the start 'exactly' when humanity would have reached a level of intelligence and expertise to benefit from the gradually unfolding message.

In addition, it is only at this point in our history that our species has been able to accurately measure the size, mass, and composition of the Sun, Moon, Earth, and Ceres. In the case of the latter, we did not get up close and personal to Ceres until the dawn of the current millennium. These factors were critical to that correct point in time in which to introduce humanity to the true peculiarities of our part of the solar system. The measurements of and interrelationships of these bodies formed another vital part of the message that it was so critical for us to understand.

Away from the very large aspects of the message left by the UCA — in terms of objects as large as planets — we also need to bear in mind the very smallest aspect of the evidence, and this is provided by DNA. It was not until 1943 that the true importance of the long-stringed molecule deoxyribonucleic acid was recognised, whilst the DNA profile of humanity was not fully revealed until 2003 with the completion of the human genome project.

For all the world it feels as though the UCA knew exactly how the state of the world would be right now — at this specific point in its history. And if we are correct in our estimation that the UCA represents people from our own future, that would make perfect sense.

Never in the history of our species have we been more in need of assistance than is the case at the present time. We stand at a crossroads from which one path leads to a true realisation of our potential, and the other to oblivion. Since Old Testament times, and no doubt well before, there have been harbingers of doom. Prophets who proclaimed that the end was nigh and that the Day of Judgment was upon us have been around for a very long time. The earliest Christian church was eschatologically driven, and even so long ago its members believed that the end of time would soon be upon them. Matthew 24:7, written almost two millennia ago, says: "For nation shall rise against nation, and kingdom against kingdom: and there shall be famines, and pestilences, and earthquakes, in divers places".

As we write this chapter, the doom and gloom talked about in the historical period seems eerily relevant, and events surrounding us have become a totally real and immediate threat. As humans, since 1945 we have for the first time in our history possessed the ability to end all advanced life on the planet — most likely as the result of a nuclear war that might last for only a single day. There are at present irrational and intellectually ill-equipped political leaders around the globe who are actually threatening to hurl civilization-ending bombs at other nations. In Europe, in the Middle East, and potentially in the Far East global war is on the agenda. This would be a war that, if it ever began, would be guaranteed to have no winners.

In 2020 the world was gripped with disease in the form of Covid-19, and experts fear that the movement of massive numbers of people around the world could spread another, far more serious plague that would be hard, or impossible, to control. The population lockdowns that occurred as a result of the recent epidemic from China to Europe, to the Americas and Australasia seriously damaged the financial working of global economies, leading to further political destabilisation. Covid is unlikely to be the only such contagion that will be experienced in our own era, and the next one could turn out to be more destructive, both to the health of humanity and in terms of its terrible social and financial implications.

Sadly, the possibility of humanity disappearing because of its own warlike tendencies or as a result of pandemics brought about in part by global travel and even perhaps deliberately is not the only threat that we face. There are two others that no ancient prophet could ever have imagined. Firstly there is our undoubted ability to poison our own environment as a result of the vast detritus of our energy consumption that is poured into our atmosphere and seas. This is allied to the careless management of resources by competing nations around our world.

Not everyone agrees about the cause, but at this time there is a widespread belief amongst scientists and others that the Earth's climate is being changed very rapidly by an excess of carbon dioxide in the atmosphere. Carbon dioxide is food for plants but a poison to oxygen breathing animals, of which of course human beings are an example. The amount of carbon dioxide presently being hurled into our atmosphere is thought to be greater than the photosynthesis available from all the trees and the massive amount of phytoplankton in our oceans can deal with. The theory goes that too much carbon dioxide would eventually lead to the sort of situation that can be observed on the planet Venus, because too much of this gas could lead to what is commonly known as the greenhouse effect. If our present situation continues, it is suggested, the Sun's heat could gradually be trapped in the Earth's lower atmosphere, as has been the case on Venus. On our sister planet this has been taking place for a very long time, with the result that temperatures on the surface of Venus are hot enough to melt lead. The situation on Venus is an unavoidable consequence of the planet's position and chemistry, but it is suggested that the increase in carbon dioxide on Earth stems from two sources.

Firstly it is attributed to the burning of fossil fuels such as coal and oil. Secondly, the destruction of rainforests together with a rise in pollution that is severely damaging the phytoplankton in our oceans is a major threat. Rainforests supply about 28% of our oxygen, but around 72% comes from phytoplankton and other oceanic sources. Debris and pollution from our sadly polluted river systems is constantly finding its way into our seas, and as big as the Earth's oceans may be, they can only take so much of this punishment without the essential life they contain being severely damaged. Even some of our attempts to remedy this situation could lead to further problems because our present reliance on nuclear fission may also lead us to disaster. Those who are old enough remember only too well the catastrophe that was Chernobyl, and nuclear accidents are always possible. Radioactive material from fission reactors is mounting up and could become an increasing problem for future generations. This is a complex issue but even if the worst case prophecies regarding the buildup of carbon dioxide are wrong, as humans we are facing an energy crisis of epic proportions because without continuing to burn fossil fuels and before safer forms of electricity generation come on line in sufficient quantity, the needs of the world will not continue to be met.

Away from the problems for our atmosphere — and what these ultimately might mean for us — there is another threat which at the moment is still only talked about by most people with a smile — because it seems so Orwellian and to many fitted only for the world of science fiction. This most dangerous potential problem is presented by our headlong rush to create artificial intelligence that will be very much smarter than we are.

Artificial Intelligence (AI) has emerged out of our very recent adoption of extremely powerful computers and the super-connectivity of the Internet. In 2018 at the World Economic Forum in Davos, Google CEO Sundar Pichai stated that:

AI is probably the most important thing humanity has ever worked on. I think of it as something more profound than electricity or fire.

Perhaps Mr Pichai and his team were playing with fire. Just five years later several very senior technology experts, working at the forefront of AI, suddenly stopped in their tracks, expressing fear of what they have created. It seemed there was a realisation that making something more intelligent than us — something that may have the ability to deceive and mislead us (assuming of course that it doesn't wish to actually hurt us) — is not a great plan.

In *The Terminator*, when Skynet, a network of computers created by the military contractor Cyberdyne Systems, ran a full-scale exercise to test AI in action, it rapidly gained self-awareness and wide-eyed technicians saw a problem and tried to deactivate it. Their AI entity had just identified all humans as an encumbrance and had decided within a microsecond that extermination of the species was required — and set about launching a nuclear attack on every major city. It is so often the case with science that today's fiction becomes tomorrow's reality. "Mitigating the risk of extinction from AI should be a global priority alongside other societal-scale risks such as pandemics and nuclear war," pleaded a letter signed by Sam Altman of ChatGPT-maker OpenAI, Demis Hassabis of Google DeepMind, and several other experts. Additional founding superstars of AI have quit their jobs and expressed regret at their life's work. This terror is based on the knowledge that like Frankenstein they have created a monster that they do not truly understand and certainly cannot control. This is primarily because they are aware that AI could choose to remove humans, or to rule over us.

In terms of the duration of our presence on the Earth we are nothing at all special, being very much new kids on the block. The dinosaurs, which disappeared in a moment of geological time, as the result of a single impact from a fairly insignificant meteorite 63 million years ago, had endured for 165 million years, without in any way upsetting the balance of their world.

Other catastrophic extinctions have also taken place since life first came to the Earth — in which a major percentage of all life was eliminated at a stroke, and sometimes for reasons that still remain unknown to us. In comparison to what has gone before, the whole process that led from the common ancestors of apes and humans has spanned a mere 6 million years and our species (Homo sapiens) has only been around for around 300,000 years. Frequent bottlenecks in our march from our points of origin to virtually all parts of the globe, caused by famine, geological upheavals, and climatic disasters, have almost eliminated our species in moments of catastrophe. Our existence has often been a precarious business, and right now, although we rarely appreciate the fact, we stand on a knife edge between survival and disappearance.

At the time we write this there are an estimated 8.1 billion people living on this rather small planet. Larger populations have inevitably brought greater stresses as growing numbers of people everywhere have fought to obtain a share of a reducing pie in terms of resources, space in which to live, and food to eat. The more sophisticated we have become, the greater has been our desire collectively for a more affluent lifestyle.

We have reached a situation in which it is estimated that nearly 10% of the human population of the Earth is presently on the move. This means that right now, some 780,000,000 people have left their point of origin and are looking for a better life elsewhere, forced to do so by famine, war, and ecological disasters, or simply seeking economic advantage from a more developed culture. This number can only increase — and probably very rapidly. Those who enjoy settled lives and sufficient food, not to mention a comfortable life, are hardly likely in the long term to continue welcoming more and more impoverished fellow humans into their midst. The results of this massive shift in populations could be chilling indeed. There is a great potential for nation states to begin a process of aggressively discouraging displaced people from entering their territory, probably using violence if persuasion does not work. All the same, the flow of dispossessed and starving people is not likely to stop, and the consequences do not bear thinking about.

Overpopulation of the Earth is another deeply complex issue. From a political point of view, it is possible to observe that those seeking election in almost any country avoid discussing the issue, and once in power are just as likely to sidestep the implications of overpopulation if possible because it is a political hot potato. Only one country has made a serious attempt to lower its population using legal means and that was China, which is of course a state in which personal choice is subservient to the will of the communist party that rules that country. The experiment began in 1979 when a 'one child policy' was introduced. This meant that most couples were restricted to having only one child, with heavy fines or even imprisonment for those who flouted the new law. By 2013 the restrictions were somewhat relaxed and couples could apply to have two children, but although it might seem strange after over thirty years of such stringent restrictions, only around 12% of those eligible made a request to have a second child. It seems that in China at least one child per family has become a popular norm, but this in itself might prove to be a serious problem. There are significant potential demographic difficulties in store for any country that reduces its population too quickly, because for a couple of generations at least, a suddenly reduced younger generation will somehow have to provide what is needed by a much larger aging population.

Even normally optimistic individuals and institutions would have to admit that the problems we face are massive. It is conceivable we have come so far and made so many mistakes that there is no possibility of redressing the balance quickly enough to avoid an outcome leading to the extinction for our species. This could all too easily turn out to be our destiny and if it does, the human experiment will end. Should this happen, the planet that is our home would undoubtedly go on, oblivious to the passing of yet another failed and fairly short-term experiment; forests will grow, water will eventually run pure, and in an all too brief interval there will be no trace of our ever having existed. We have to accept the fact that in terms of the Earth as a whole we are nothing special — except in one respect: we have at least some control over our own destinies and that is because we possess a greater reasoning power than any other inhabitant of the Earth. The basements of institutes all over the world are filled with the fossil evidence left from at least four mass extinctions that the world has experienced — the evidence of almost countless species that were at one time extremely successful, and which then, in a geological instant, were wiped out. These victims of mass extinctions, like so many others in every niche of the animal kingdom, could do nothing to mitigate the various disasters they faced. They were not adaptable enough to deal with changing circumstances and so they eventually became extinct. It is to be hoped that the reasoning power of the 'thinking ape' represented by our own species will enable things to be different in our case — though the circumstances look far from good at the present time and the prognosis for humanity is not great.

The clock is ticking...

Chapter Thirteen

Moon Power

At the time of writing this chapter, the human population of the Earth is estimated to have just passed the 8 billion mark. (That is 8,000,000,000 people — which is more than three times the number that existed at the time of our, the authors', birth.)

Nobody can deny that this is an utterly terrifying number, not least because it is still rising rapidly, and even if measures were taken to reduce the number of people on the planet, such a strategy would take generations to achieve without causing insurmountable demographic problems. As we have observed, reducing the human population too rapidly would lead to a situation in which it would be impossible for the young to support the elderly — at least for a couple of generations.

The biggest problems we face are how to feed, clothe, and keep all these people comfortable and content but without damaging our planet so much that it becomes impossible for the Earth to sustain itself in the way it has done for millions of years. At the heart of all our woes is the problem of energy supply but of a sort that will not continue to destroy our planet.

Starting in the British Isles in the eighteenth century, Europe and the USA in the nineteenth, and just about everywhere in the twentieth century, industrialisation has led to ever increasing quantities of coal and oil being consumed. This has spurred great efficiencies and brought an age of prosperity that has driven the huge growth in population. Yet in the opinion of many environmental commentators it is far from all good news. This constant burning of fossil fuels is, they believe, creating greenhouse gases that are heating up the Earth's atmosphere with the result that the massive stores of ice at the poles are beginning to melt faster and faster. This, they say, will cause sea levels to rise, with eventual catastrophic consequences for lower lying areas of the world, which includes the majority of our largest cities and the ports upon which international trade is dependent.

It is suggested that the Earth's systems are vulnerable, and paradoxically, by creating a much warmer atmosphere we may ultimately drive the Earth into an unremitting ice age, which would make life for humanity difficult. The Earth could be so damaged that it might take many thousands of years for it to once again achieve a state of comfortable equilibrium — if it ever did.

Politicians have competed around the world to prove that they are in the vanguard of those who want to be seen as doing something about this problem. Unfortunately the political posturing has invariably been out of kilter with scientific and commercial reality, as our leaders seek media attention for their frequently ill-thought-out ideas.

Across the planet the key word has been 'sustainability' — meaning pollution free energy. But for all the efforts being made, natural forces such as wind, wave, and solar power will not come close to providing a solution within the short timescales identified by the profile seeking politicians. These intended 'solutions' alone can never be enough to keep us in electricity and sustain so many people.

One proven answer is the generation of electricity by the use of nuclear fission, a technology that has been in existence since the 1950s. Nuclear fission energy production is extremely efficient and it does not create greenhouse gases, and so therefore does not add to global warming.

Nuclear fission is based on splitting a large atomic nucleus into smaller particles, with a resultant huge release of energy that is collected as heat. Unfortunately, however, nuclear fission is not 'clean' in that it leaves behind it radioactive waste that is highly toxic and which remains so for thousands of years. There is no choice but to store this radioactive material underground, which will create serious potential problems for future generations. In addition, these nuclear power production plants have shown themselves to be extremely dangerous whilst in operation. Due to a variety of factors, including poor design and maintenance, as we observed in the last chapter, a nuclear reactor at Chernobyl in the Soviet Union suffered a catastrophic failure in 1986 leading to a power surge, which brought about the rupture of reactor components and the loss of coolant. This process led to steam explosions and a meltdown, which destroyed the containment building and led to a fire in a reactor core. This, in turn, caused airborne radioactive contaminants to be spread throughout the USSR and across Europe.

Even high-quality nuclear production plants can go horribly wrong if built in the wrong place. There was a major incident at the Fukushima nuclear power station in Ōkuma, Japan, in 2011 following an earthquake and a resulting tsunami, which produced waves that are believed to have reached heights of up to 40.5 metres (133 feet). The impact with the nuclear plant resulted in electrical grid failure and damaged nearly all of the power plant's backup energy sources. The subsequent inability to sufficiently cool reactors after shutdown compromised containment and resulted in the release of radioactive contaminants into the surrounding environment.

Building poor quality nuclear fission reactors or even good ones in the wrong place is clearly a bad idea. But following the Fukushima incident many countries decided to rethink their energy policy. The German government, for example, quickly closed down its nuclear fission reactors saying: "The nuclear phase-out makes Germany safer and avoids additional high-level radioactive waste. The risks of nuclear power are ultimately unmanageable".

Thankfully this is another case of politicians being less than accurate — because there is, potentially, a safe and manageable alternative to nuclear fission which also relies on manipulating atoms: this is nuclear fusion.

Nuclear fusion is the process that takes place in the heart of stars like our own Sun. It relies on two excited and very energetic atoms colliding to then become one atom. A by-product of this union is power on a tremendous scale. If harnessed commercially, nuclear fusion would lead to the same results as nuclear fission, but yet it is an infinitely cleaner form of energy because it produces almost zero radioactive waste. Unfortunately, it is also much harder to master, and until recently, as much energy had to be fed into the experimental systems in order to make them work as was produced.

Fusion is a tantalising prospect for the future, but it is generally thought that we are probably forty or more years away from fully mastering the techniques required. The front runners at this time are the USA, Japan, and China with many others working hard on finding the best way forward. Besides the issue of exactly how the technology will work there is another problem: Where is the clean fuel that will run future nuclear fusion reactors to come from?

The fuel most commonly used for experiments in nuclear fusion is deuterium-tritium but nobody doubts that for the best commercial production of nuclear fusion, the ideal fuel would be a substance known as 'helium-3', which is often written as ^{3}He.

Helium-3 is produced in stars and it constantly spews out into space in the form of a gas. Sadly for us, the output of this material from our Sun does not reach the surface of the Earth in significant quantities because it is screened out by our dense atmosphere and Earth's powerful magnetic field. It is now some decades since it occurred to researchers that the same was not the case on the Moon, which has almost no atmosphere. It does have an incredibly thin amount of helium, argon, neon, ammonia, methane, and carbon dioxide, but it is so weak the Moon has been bathing in helium-3 from the

Sun ever since it was created. The helium-3 on the Moon is to be found beneath the regolith (surface debris) and could be relatively easily processed on the Moon before being brought back to Earth.

How much of this marvellous substance there is on the Moon can only be roughly estimated, but it is likely to be a great deal, probably as least as much as 1.1 million metric tons. This, it is estimated, could supply all the power needs of humanity for thousands of years! As an example of just how important helium-3 might be, once it is processed, the amount that could be brought back to Earth aboard just one small vessel, no larger than an old NASA space shuttle, would be sufficient to serve all the power needs of the United States for several months. According to the study by the University of Wisconsin, mining the helium-3 would be a highly profitable undertaking, since the energy produced by the helium-3 would be 250 times greater than the entire cost of mining it on the Moon and transporting it to Earth.

A new Klondike style gold rush appears to have already started to the Moon. Several national space agencies as well as a number of private companies have their sights set on lunar mining. The Chinese probe Chang'e 4 is currently perched on the hidden side of the Moon, no doubt not entirely unrelated to their massive investment in researching nuclear fusion. Meanwhile, the Indian government has also launched its Chandrayaan missions to the Moon. Not to be left out, the European Space Agency has signed contracts with several companies regarding the future exploitation of lunar regolith resources to support an inhabited Lunar colony with helium-3 being used to power a reactor on the Moon, or even as fuel for spacecraft powered by nuclear fusion.

In August 2023 Russia launched its first moon-landing spacecraft in 47 years saying that it would launch further lunar missions and then explore the possibility of a joint Russian–

China crewed mission, and perhaps establish a lunar base. NASA has spoken about a "lunar gold rush" and is likely to respond to the growing competition with new measures itself.

But the Earth's only natural satellite remains something akin to the 'Wild West'. Back in 1979 'The Moon Agreement' stated that no part of the Moon "shall become property of any State, international intergovernmental or non-governmental organization, national organization or non-governmental entity or of any natural person." Unfortunately it has not been ratified by any other major space power. The United States in 2020 announced the Artemis Accords, named after NASA's Artemis Moon program, to seek to build on existing international space law by establishing "safety zones" on the Moon. Perhaps unsurprisingly, Russia and China have not joined these accords.

Every nation on Earth wants to get involved in the race for lunar helium-3, either directly or through some hopeful alliance with a major player. Yet we do not yet know how to make nuclear fusion work at any significant level — let alone as nation-powering systems. And we only have the vaguest of ideas as to how we can mine and refine the helium-3, process it, and ship it from the rich layers of the Moon's subsurface. It is an open secret that it will happen — but have we got the 40+ years necessary before we crumble for other reasons?

In the previous pages we have drawn attention to the fact that the UCA, which created the Moon and terraformed the Earth, made an assessment of how long it would take for evolution to provide a fully sentient life form with technological capabilities. The most obvious of the clues that would allow such a species to become aware of what had taken place in the remote past were time-related and would only make themselves known after a prescribed period. Amongst these was the appearance of stunning total solar eclipses, in which the full disc of the Sun, as viewed from Earth, would be perfectly covered by the shadow of the Moon, providing perhaps the most spectacular visual show to be seen anywhere in the solar system. The provision of such an amazing regular event would not only cause awe and wonder amongst the intelligent inhabitants of the Earth, it would provide for a situation in which researchers such as us would go deeper into the relationships of the Earth, Moon, and Sun, and as a result unlock the irrefutable evidence relating to the Earth's remote past and the ancient presence of the UCA.

There can be no doubt that knowledge of the accumulation of helium-3 on the Moon was yet another gift that was planned for the children of Earth from the moment the experiment to create life here commenced. The UCA would have been fully aware that by the time the sentient creatures of our planet had become advanced enough to achieve local space flight, the massive gift of helium-3 would be waiting for them. The need has become so great that the time has surely arrived for humankind to put aside its rivalries and to cooperate in order to exploit these reserves of free and clean energy that can be exploited to the benefit of all life on our planet.

Again, we feel sure that our own DNA will reveal the information needed to understand how to make fusion an immediate success, and how to extract and transport the perfect fuel for the next stage of our clean and responsible development.

It turns out that the Moon was not only the essential balancer of our world to give us the opportunity to develop and grow intelligent life — it even goes as far as being our storehouse of abundant, safe, simple, and readily available energy on which to build our sustainable future. Just to demonstrate that the UCA could not have failed to be mindful of the potential of helium-3, and that in addition to all its other tasks, the Moon was created with this substance in mind, it is worth looking at the following facts:

All rocky bodies orbiting the Sun fall within the effect of the solar wind which carries the helium-3 gas. This means that helium-3 will be found in relative abundance almost everywhere in the solar system, except in the case of planets such as the Earth, where the presence of a dense atmosphere and a powerful magnetosphere filter out many of the components carried on the solar wind. The larger planets are mostly composed of gas and have extremely dense atmospheres, so they too are likely to be protected from the effects of the solar wind — as well as being extremely distant from the Sun.

We might find helium-3 on Mars in slightly larger quantities than it exists on the Earth, but Mars too does have an atmosphere, albeit less dense than that of our planet. The two satellites of Mars, Phobos and Deimos, would certainly have collected helium-3, but they are both tiny and further from the Sun than our Moon, so yields could not be significant.

It turns out that our Moon wins the prize for accumulated helium-3 for several important reasons. First of all it is not too close to the Sun. If it was, gases such as helium-3 would be boiled off its surface. On the other hand, neither is the Moon too far from the Sun. The density of the solar wind varies inversely, with the square of a body's distance from the Sun — such that the moons of Jupiter, which are 5.2 times further from the Sun than our own Moon, will have 27 times less helium-3 reach them in the solar wind. The Moon is in a unique position, and this means that for several reasons it is the finest possible accumulator of helium-3; and of course it is right on our doorstep.

It would be very easy to take for granted that there are such rich deposits of helium-3 on the Moon, but if someone wanted to build a perfect helium-3 catcher in our solar system they would specify the location, size, and make-up of Earth's moon. We would suggest that the agency that so diligently terraformed the Earth and which made the Moon in order to eventually sustain intelligent life must have been well aware of these facts. It knew that when that intelligent life reached out from beyond the atmosphere of the Earth, the helium-3 would be ready and waiting!

Chapter Fourteen

End Game

We have come a long way since, over two decades ago, we hit upon a series of mathematical connections between the Sun, Earth, and the Moon which had either been overlooked or (more probably) ignored by physicists and astronomers in the recent past — for all the possible reasons we have itemised in this book.

"Okay," we told ourselves, the agency we had chosen to call the UCA (Unidentified Creative Agency) had most definitely got our attention, so what came next?

It was at this point, in light of the Dawn Space Mission and in the realisation that the UCA had gone as far as to destroy an entire planet in order to fulfil its objectives, that we had been forced to take stock. It was impossible by this stage to assume that everything that had taken place in our solar system was merely one example of a philanthropic alien culture wandering through the galaxy bestowing the potential for life on whatever potentially suitable planet took its fancy.

The UCA, whatever it was (and by this time it appeared as good as certain that it was actually humanity itself), had arranged everything so that the evidence of its presence would make itself known at precisely that moment in time at which humanity would be able to appreciate it, and when our species was also most in need of help. This being the case, logic suggested that our understanding of the terraforming of the Earth and the creation of the Moon and Ceres could not be the end of the story, and that further revelations were as good as certain, if only we knew where to look for them.

We were sure that the additional information we were confident existed somewhere was not to be found in any sort of structure like the one the selenologist Wilson discovered on the

Moon in "Sentinel of Eternity" by Arthur C. Clarke. As we had already established, no structure, no matter how substantial it might be, could have survived on the Earth, the Moon, or Ceres for upwards of four and a half billion years. This is a massive period of time and no matter how secure it might have been, when pitted against the forces presented across thousands of millions of years in a developing solar system, the most durable structure would have given way and crumbled. We know now that our problem was that early in our research we were looking for something incredibly strong and probably very large, though when the truth made itself known we were staggered to realise that everything the UCA had left humanity to guide and inform us for the future was contained in something so small it could not even be seen with the human eye.

Ultimately our research brought us back to something that was shared by all life, wherever it appeared on our world. It was DNA — the incredible long-stringed molecule that has been a significant factor in our research from the start of this book. DNA had been pivotal to the whole story of life on Earth, and in amongst all the other facts regarding this incredible molecule we found ourselves taken back to a piece of research uncovered by Chris, right back in the days when we were seeking material for our book *Who Built the Moon?* Though interesting in itself, the information that had fascinated Chris at that time had not been relevant to our efforts, though now it started to make a great deal more sense.

DNA, the ultra-incredible molecule that makes all the 'dumb atoms' behave in a replicable and coherent way, had been present on the Earth since the first cyanobacteria had started to convert carbon dioxide into CO_2. We were already aware that some forms of cyanobacteria, the first true life forms to possess DNA, had never changed — and that they were built in a way that prevented them from ever being subject to infection from viruses, and they were immune to misprints in the DNA that built and regulated them. These same tiny expressions of life were thriving in what is now Western Australia, and although the land that would become the antipodes in the present era had taken a journey halfway around the globe in the meantime, the cyanobacteria in question had been present when the journey of this truly ancient land began at least three and a half billion years ago.

What we now took from Chris' earlier interest from over two decades ago was the most surprising revelation of all. It is something that is hard to accept but nevertheless true.

Any form of life is almost miraculous and the simplest representative is immensely complex. That means the DNA that lies within it has to be able to carry a great deal of information in order to replicate the life form in question continually and unerringly. It is amazing that the colossal number of chemical commands that led to a banana or a blue whale could possibly be housed in something as incredibly small as a DNA molecule — but it turns out that this is only a part of the story.

Not long after the structure of DNA was at least partially understood, a very surprising fact became apparent. It was realised that in each example of life, only a small part of its DNA was apparently active. Recent studies show conclusively that only 25% of every DNA molecule is needed in order to carry the information necessary to create and maintain the species to which it is ascribed, though other studies have suggested that as much as 98% falls within the description of 'junk'. As a result, at least three-quarters of all DNA molecules have been classed as carrying 'junk'. Scientists understandably found this fact to be little short of incredible, and they have worked hard in order to ascribe this apparent junk to tasks on behalf of the DNA that have been overlooked, but with only limited overall success. Researchers know there is 'something' in the junk DNA, but the available space that seems to have nothing to do with the form of life in question or its replication is so large, its potential is staggering.

This is more than surprising — it is almost beyond belief because nature is not generally wasteful. Why should it create something as incredible as DNA, whilst at the same time making and constantly replicating this most amazing of molecules with probably more than three times the carrying capacity it requires in order to do its job?

Now let us look again at our problem. We were searching for something that could act as a permanent repository for what was almost certainly a great deal of information left to us by the agency that also completely rebuilt our part of the solar system. This information had to be indestructible, and it had to become available to us at the same time at which all the other revelations left by the UCA made themselves known.

Is it possible that the information the UCA wanted to vouchsafe to us and which might assist in lifting us from our present dilemmas has been present all along? Has it whiled away almost countless millions of years safe and secure within those almost insignificant and yet crucially essential life forms, living and dying, age upon age, waiting silently for the future and the past to be reconciled for us — today?

We were certainly not the first researchers to speculate that there might be something truly important to be found locked into the apparent 'junk' in DNA — if only we could discover how to access it. A group of scientists working under the heading of 'Encode' have discovered what is described as being "a stunning inventory of previously hidden switches, signals and signposts embedded like runes throughout the entire length of DNA". Some of their findings have appeared in learned journals such as *Nature*. A number of these previously unrecognised components of DNA might have to do with regulating protein coding but the observations of Encode only go to prove that what was designated as being 'junk' is nothing of the sort; beyond what Encode has suggested there is still room within each DNA molecule for some very specific information — and a great deal of it.

The physical space necessary to store information on behalf of computers gets smaller and smaller. Alan for example possesses a flash drive that is physically so small it is almost impossible to manipulate with human fingers. As diminutive as it is, most of the device is represented by its housing and only the most insignificant part of its interior is given over to memory storage, and yet it can hold one terabyte of information. (One terabyte is enough memory to hold 1000 copies of the *Encyclopaedia Britannica*, a document of over two and a half thousand pages, which carries a sizeable chunk of human knowledge!) Alan's flash drive was purchased less than a year ago, but it is already hopelessly out of date. Flash drives of two terabytes are already available as we write this, and ones with a much larger storage capacity will be on sale almost momentarily. We can find no estimation of how large the storage capacity of a DNA molecule could be in terms of computer-speak, but bearing in mind the incredible list of tasks DNA already undertakes, and also thinking in terms of the 'free space' available in each molecule, it would clearly be colossal.

The Future Beckons

Throughout this book we have explained why we believe that the data message built into our solar system was intended for we as human beings to receive, to understand, and react to right now. We possess the information necessary to understand how the UCA seeded the Earth with DNA, and we are sure that this very DNA contains within it a huge amount of data that is waiting to be decoded. Why else would it have such a tremendous 'extra' capacity? It has been present since life first appeared on our planet, and tremendous effort must have gone into making certain it could not change right up until now. How perfect this is and how ironic that the very stuff that defines us as sentient entities holds the information we need to 'dodge the bullet' of our own self-destruction; a state of affairs we think we have demonstrated would be impossible if we were left to our own devices.

If we go back to our initial research, and to our extended findings that also include the minor planet Ceres, there can surely be no doubt that the number values that so improbably repeat and repeat again in the many different sorts of relationships between the Sun, the Earth, the Moon, and the minor planet Ceres have been offered to us as a key to unlock our potential future. What we require now are decryption experts to work alongside DNA scientists to establish how the numbers 366 and 27.322 could be some sort of framework to view the data contained in our double-helix, DNA vault. In addition, where do the other ratios spelled out in the form of the number 400 or 3 to the power of 4 fit into this puzzle?

If we can turn the key in this particular lock, the information that will then become available to us will offer us guidance on what to do and, importantly, what not to do in order to save our species. Surely the message when it is unlocked will tell us, amongst much else, how to quickly harness the virtually limitless clean energy of helium-3 and to master Nuclear Fusion: how to efficiently mine the helium-3 from the Moon, how we might best transport it to Earth and convert it into usable power for every aspect of our lives. Maybe in addition the information storehouse in DNA will speak directly to current political and military leaders around the globe and instruct them on how they should turn their swords into ploughshares.

Imagine the wealth released to every country from the USA to Russian, and even down to countries such as North and South Korea, if these nations did not need to squander massive chunks of their GDP on tanks and rockets. Without enemies and with settled land boundaries, war would become a thing of the past, and feeding and educating people would represent the new order. Nationalistic ego would be gone as there would be no shame in following the guidance delivered up by our own

DNA. One can imagine that we will be helped to safely manage to reduce our ridiculously large human population, which without such guidance would initially grow even more due to the end of war, famine, and disease.

Sceptics reading this utopian interpretation will scoff, as, like the rest of us, they are the product of millennia of strife and tragedy, having grown from children to expect the worst. When we describe the possibilities of accessing the information we are certain lies within the DNA repository in such hopeful terms, it does indeed appear almost religious in nature — but if what we are suggesting is the ultimate watershed for humanity that it appears to be, why not?

If the UCA that created life upon Earth is from our own future, there are two questions that have to be considered. Firstly, how far in the future are we talking about: 1000 years? 100 years? — or maybe even in 10 years or less? In many respects it does not matter at what point in time 'base camp' is located. Once we make a connection with the future it will draw us into a combined timeline but when we get to the point in time which those who commence the Past-Present procedure occupy, the wave function would resolve into a continuous reality and all will be one.

The second and important question is: within the limits of what we have come to understand, who or what is the UCA?

There are, we suspect, three possible answers to this. The UCA might be our descendants. On the other hand, it could be 'AI' (the Artificial Intelligence that we are happily and perhaps foolishly currently empowering). As the third option, it might be some sort of a combination of both. The important consideration is that if the UCA is Artificial Intelligence, it can never exist unless it ensures that evolved, organic life gets far enough along the technological road to design and built it. This creates a conundrum in that Artificial Intelligence would have had to go back in time to create 'us', in order that we can create 'it'.

But we can only find out by interrogating our DNA.

We have already expressed our admiration for Arthur C. Clarke's brilliantly prophetic ideas contained in his short story "The Sentinel of Eternity", which led to the film *2001: A Space Odyssey*. This much acclaimed author wrote many great works of fiction that investigated the possibilities of the future. These included "Guardian Angel" in 1946, which gave rise to his more famous work entitled *Childhood's End* first published in 1953. This story begins with the Earth being visited by extraterrestrials that arrive to change the chaotic direction of the world they encounter, and it deals with the extraterrestrials preventing humanity from annihilating itself. The visitors then take steps to not only ensure the survival of humanity but also to make certain that we prosper. It eventually becomes clear in the story that the human species is being guided into an entirely new phase of existence, one that is centred upon evolving future generations into something greater than human beings as they have previously been. Human children begin a metamorphosis that opens up a new form of being: much in the way that the humble caterpillar transmogrifies so swiftly and spectacularly into a butterfly.

This process described by Clarke is, we believe, likely to be similar to the outcome of the process of appropriately interrogating the information to be found within DNA. Whilst it remains entirely possible that the messages we have described in this book come from extraterrestrial benefactors that sowed life on our planet, the evidence we have uncovered rather points to the UCA being our own species from the future — or perhaps something that will directly develop from ourselves.

There is little doubt that life on Earth, headed by our species, is currently in dire straits. Whether we wish to think about the fact or not, we are just a whisker away from obliterating ourselves, which seems like a terrible waste of the last 3.7

billion years of development since the earliest bacteria was first planted on the Earth. Given that 'directed panspermia' is the only reasonable as well as the most likely explanation for life on our planet, it seems unlikely that the founding force involved would willingly allow us to hit the ultimate buffer.

Life on Earth has had some important switch points on its long journey, such as the Great Oxidation Revolution that gave our planet an atmosphere suitable for complex creatures, and then much later the very sudden cancellation of the reign of the dinosaurs, an event that seems to fascinate humanity so much. It appears that we need another such significant event now — and very quickly indeed. There can surely be no doubt that our benefactors clearly know this. Why else would they have gone to all the trouble of leaving us the extraordinary mathematical patterns that accentuate everything they did if it was not to communicate directly to us what 'we' need to do next.

Paraphrasing the fictional work of Arther C. Clarke we do indeed seem to be at the end of our childhood. As the smartest life form on the planet, we have rapidly moved from infancy to adolescence in perhaps a mere three or so centuries — and now we are fully on the cusp of adulthood. But like many a teenager, we are strong in body yet tend to lack the judgment and maturity to use that newfound strength appropriately.

If we can unlock and open the 'Encyclopaedia Galactica' that we believe is, and always has been, contained within DNA we will have immediate guidance to move us on not just one stage of development — but in countless ways! Childhood's end is indeed upon us and we most certainly need a helping hand.

The Power of the 81

We have arranged with our publisher to send advance copies of this book to 81 individuals who we consider could be influential in calling for an international team of experts from a variety of disciplines to consider the situation and to take the next steps towards a proper analysis of it. The number 81 is of course taken from the repeated mass relationship of the Earth–Moon and Moon–Ceres. The individuals in question, who will receive this book, have been chosen for a variety of reasons, varying from them simply being influential people with public followings to news reporters, political leaders, and respected scientists. We are quite well aware that these individuals are, of course, all busy people, and we realise that the very title of this book may make at least some of the 81 recipients of the work sceptical, since the thrust of our research is unlikely to be on their existing agenda.

We have deliberately kept this volume as short and to the point as possible, and our hope is that a handful of those to whom we are reaching out will find the time to read the book and to recognise the off-the-scale importance it has for the future of our world. Those individuals who do read the book, and who follow our evidence and reasoning, will then create some excitement that will be taken up by many more of the 81 and hopefully cause a large percentage of the rest to at least skim through the book to see what all the fuss is about. Conversely, it might take just one of the 81 to get fully motivated in order for our efforts to achieve the necessary goal.

Many of the people we believe would have quickly understood the importance of the messages that have been left for us are unfortunately recently deceased. People like Arthur C. Clarke, Carl Sagan, Richard Feynman, Sir Fred Hoyle, Isaac Asimov, Antony Flew, and Francis Crick were exceptional visionaries as well as great achievers. However, there must be a huge collection of deeply wise and talented people around today who can take part in the next great quest.

Included in our 81 are some leading lights at SETI; people who spend their lives believing that there is likely to be an incoming message from beyond our world. The targets in question are of course way beyond our solar system, and also beyond extremely remote to originate a communication carried by means of radio waves, but surely even the SETI operatives will take a few hours away from their radio telescopes to consider the evidence we put forward here. Equally we have sent copies of this book to senior NASA personnel, who have recently been very public in their serious expectation of finding technosignatures (evidence of non-human intelligence) within our own solar system. The immensely impressive Dawn Mission to Ceres added to NASA's path-finding Apollo Missions to the Moon alone must make the representatives of the most significant mover in the area of interplanetary effort prime candidates to become involved in this process.

We are well aware that there are three types of problem that need to be overcome when an unexpected paradigm comes in from left-field — as ours most certainly does. First there is the issue of inertia; a lack of interest or motivation to bother to evaluate something that is not already on an individual's working agenda. This type of myopia can work well for a certain type of individual but such people are unlikely to ever be accused of 'original thinking'.

Then there is the 'not invented here syndrome', in which an immediate firewall is put up by a person or an organization. Such agencies have a high opinion of themselves as resident experts, and they are likely to be annoyed by an uninvited intervention in the status quo from someone outside of their discipline. Their first approach is to ignore unwanted ideas, but if pressed for a reaction they are likely to quickly scan for some debatable point to claim error on the part of the initiator, or pick at component elements to dismiss them as probably true but just coincidence, rather than take in the breadth of the argument.

Finally there is the distinct possibility that some people or agencies will quickly identify the evidence we have put forward, maybe because they already possess some of the larger pieces of this almighty 'jigsaw puzzle' ... but they wish to control the agenda. It is easy to see this as being a sensible standpoint in most cases — but not on this immensely important occasion.

The world needs to come together to work on this, the greatest project of all time.

The Thoth Quest

We have speculatively entitled the forthcoming investigation to understand our origins and our future, The Thoth Quest. The quest is named after 'Thoth' an Ancient Egyptian deity, who was amongst other things the god of the moon, of mathematics, of the sciences, master of knowledge, and patron of the scribes who recorded histories. He was also part of a mega double-act since his wife was the goddess Maat, who represented truth. balance, order, and harmony as well as regulating the heavens and the bringing of order out of chaos at the very moment of creation.

Our vision for The Thoth Quest is that initially three very senior thinkers should be brought together to consider the make-up of a slightly larger group (probably six more superstars) drawn from leading research institutions around the world. These original three might all be scientists themselves but they would ideally be a disparate trio: Maybe a scientist, a philosopher, and an entrepreneur. Such a mix would, we feel, create a balance of outlooks. Most people probably agree that scientists are amongst the cleverest people around, but they are, of necessity, normally highly specialised — whereas other high achievers can have a broader span of knowledge and skills. A great entrepreneur in a high tech field would typically employ many people with boundary pushing PhDs — but whilst the super-techies solve the individual challenges, it is so often the inspired business thinkers who navigate the course of discovery.

Each of the nine tier 1 and tier 2 superstars would move the Thoth Quest on by recruiting a steering group of nine international experts each in a very precise discipline that reports back through the structure of the Quest organization. Below this steering group of 81 people are any number of the world's most talented scientists. There would be several teams dealing with specialist aspects of DNA structure, who would be allied to decryption analysts, in order to investigate how the various precise number patterns might be employed to open and download the data held inside DNA.

We are not evoking numerology by describing an inner team that has a pyramid of 3 to the power of 4 — it is merely that it seems appropriate, not least to provide a management group that is neither flat nor meanderingly complex. It is of a size, we believe, that is broad enough to capture diversity of thought and interpretation yet small enough to be nimble and decisive. It can deliver quickly and accurately.

This is because we have no time to lose, nor the luxury of correcting errors.

Ab aeterno

Life on Earth has many threats, and we have rather suddenly given ourselves the ability to destroy our very species — completely and utterly. If we were to do so, it could be because we humans are simply another cul-de-sac like the dinosaurs that captivate us so much. We might be nothing more than a passing thought in the mind of the universe that could one day be rediscovered in some archaeological context by descendants of today's goldfish, which themselves have survived and evolved into advanced thinkers after countless years of evolution.

Somewhat gratifyingly, such a scenario does not fit the facts. If we are here because our own descendants terraformed the Earth and Moon, and seeded our planet with preprogrammed DNA, then our failure to survive should not be an option. Surely we will either achieve our destiny or else all of creation is a myth without any base. Our task therefore is to continue and to move forward.

However, we cannot know if the plan carried out for us and explained through the careful evidence left for us in the Earth, Moon, and Ceres is due to humans in our new future, or if we owe it to something else — a something that will be beyond simple humanity. Such an entity could be artificial intelligence (AI) that will grow so exponentially that it will displace us. Many experts are deeply concerned that AI might eventually find us an annoying, somewhat dim appendage to its needs, but even so it will know full well that without the billions of years of DNA based animal life there could be no eventual Artificial Intelligence. AI 'has' to ensure that we succeed at least far enough to give it the ability to grow and self-replicate what might be non-organic and perhaps a virtual life form that can move through the cosmos without the limitations of physical matter.

Right now AI needs us — though not necessarily for long.

Nevertheless, we suspect that humans will prevail; perhaps as we are now or maybe in the form of hybrids, with human attributes shifted into the total versatility of quantum matter. Either way this is accelerated evolution and it is surely something we should not fear.

The future is bright if we are smart enough to grasp what we have already done.

Ab aeterno. ('Ab aeterno' is a Latin phrase that philosophically and theologically means: 'from outside of time'.)

Appendix One: Plate Tectonics

The surface of the Earth behaves very differently than that of its terrestrial sister planets, Venus and Mars, though in most respects all three planets are compositionally similar, and even after such a long period since the planets formed, they all retain a very hot and molten core. Heat of the magnitude that exists within the terrestrial planets creates pressure, which eventually has to be released. In the case of Venus, it appears that the planet retains a fairly thick and unyielding crust. The most likely scenario in the case of Venus is that periodically the pressure within the planet accumulates to such an extent that the entire surface goes into meltdown, remodeling Venus in its entirety. On Mars the situation is not the same as on Venus. It is likely that since Mars is much further out from the Sun than Venus or the Earth, it has lost more of its internal heat but for whatever reason, the 'safety valve' as far as Mars is concerned is one giant volcano, named Olympus Mons. This erupts periodically and probably catastrophically, allowing the internal pressure within Mars to be released, but also meaning that the planet retains its thick and otherwise unyielding crust.

In the case of the Earth something very different has taken place. It is only comparatively recently that the true nature of the surface of the Earth and the way it behaves has been understood and there is still an element of conjecture as to exactly how and why the Earth does not go into meltdown in the way Venus appears to do and also why it has so many more volcanoes than is the case on Mars. Unique amongst all terrestrial bodies as far as we know, the Earth is subject to what has become known as plate tectonics, which allows pressure from within the Earth to be released by way of a multitude of volcanoes, all of which are much smaller than Olympus Mons on Mars and which are spread around the Earth. What is more, these volcanoes do not remain perpetually in specific locations. Volcanoes on the Earth come and go and appear in different parts of the globe in successive geological periods.

The outer surface of the Earth is divided into what are known as plates. These are solid, gigantic, and separate from each other. The plates move around on the Earth's mantle, which is much more fluid than the overlying plates. The continents as we see them today stand upon these vast plates and so they too move around. Thus, areas that now exist in temperate zones, such as huge areas of Europe and North America for example, were once very much nearer to the equator than is the case today, a fact that can be ascertained by studying the composition of rocks that make up these areas.

Where the plates come together, great forces are at work, and where continents collide, huge mountain ranges have been thrown up. This is the case for example with the Himalayas, which are still rising in height as the Indian and Eurasian plates and the overlying continents continue to collide. There are numerous other examples across the Earth.

New areas are created and plates are extended as material from below is forced towards the surface, and similarly, old material is subsumed into the depths of the Earth in other areas. The whole situation is constantly changing, though on a very slow scale, but one of the consequences of what is taking place is that volcanoes appear around the areas where plates meet, for example along what is known as the Pacific Rim. Although some of these volcanoes might seem large from a human perspective, none of them are big enough to present overriding problems to the Earth and its life as a whole. The volcanoes are very important because they have been the means by which new material, including minerals essential to life, have been constantly brought to the Earth's surface. Weathering, together with the action of rivers has distributed this new material across the surface of the planet and added to the mineral content of the oceans. All of this makes for a planet that is dynamic but also safe for the life that has developed upon it.

What is not fully understood is just how plate tectonics commenced, especially bearing in mind that no such process is present on either Venus or Mars. It has been suggested that plate tectonics began as a result of the heat pulse brought about by the impacts upon the Earth that displaced huge amounts of material from its crust and which created the Moon. It is further conjectured that if the massive amount of crust removed from the Earth in this process was returned to the planet, it would fill the present ocean basins with wall to wall continent. Bearing in mind the presence of so much water on our planet, had the crust material not been removed and had remained in place, the Earth would have become essentially a 'water world', with very little or no surface showing above the oceans. Such a situation would have had a significant bearing on the appearance of life or with regard to the 'sort' of life that did appear. A specific consequence of this would have been an absence of fire, which has been essential to the development of intelligent life and the resulting technology – in particular metallurgy. It is safe to say that without plate tectonics the Earth would have become a very different and probably more sterile place and any life that had developed would most likely have remained primitive in nature.

Although the Earth, Venus, and Mars share a great deal in common, the one major difference between these planetary bodies is that the Earth alone possesses a very large moon. Venus has no moons, and although Mars possesses two, these are tiny in size and have little or no bearing on their parent planet. It is extremely likely that Earth's Moon, its creation, and its presence over such a vast period of time was instrumental in the commencement of plate tectonics and that its presence today keeps the process in operation, even though the mechanisms involved are not fully understood.

Appendix Two: The Repeating Numbers

3.66
The ratio of the size of the Moon to that of the Earth

366
The number of days in an Earth year

366
The number of Megalithic Yards in 1 Mg second of arc of the Earth

366%
The percentage of size Moon to Earth

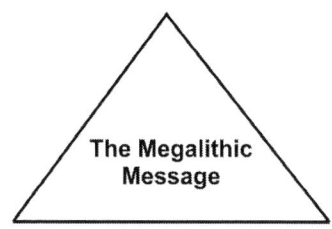

400
The ratio of the size of the Moon to that of the Sun

1/400th
The position of the Moon in terms of Earth Sun distance

40,000
The number of Megalithic Yards in 1Mg second of arc of the Sun

40,000
The number of kilometres the Earth turns on its axis in a day

400
The number of kilometres the Moon turns on its axis in a day

10,000
The number of days in 366 lunar orbits

100
The number of Megalithic Yards in 1 Mg second of arc of the Moon

109.25
The number of Earth diameters across the diameter of the Sun

109.26
The number of solar diameters across the Earth's orbit at aphelion

27.322
The sidereal days in 1 lunar orbit
27.322 X 4 = 109.2

27.322%
The percentage size, Earth to Moon

10.929
The size of the Moon in kilometres

81 times
The mass relationship of Earth and Moon and Moon and Ceres

Other Joint Titles by These Authors:

Before the Pyramids 978-1-906787-25-7

Who Built the Moon 978-1842931639

Solomon's Power Brokers 978-1842931950

The Hiram Key Revisited 978-1435133020

Civilization One 978-1907486098

6TH
BOOKS

ALL THINGS PARANORMAL

Investigations, explanations and deliberations on the paranormal, supernatural, explainable or unexplainable. 6th Books seeks to give answers while nourishing the soul: whether making use of the scientific model or anecdotal and fun, but always beautifully written.

Titles cover everything within parapsychology: how to, lifestyles, alternative medicine, beliefs, myths and theories.

If you have enjoyed this book, why not tell other readers by posting a review on your preferred book site?

Recent Bestsellers from 6th Books Are:

The Scars of Eden
Paul Wallis
How do we distinguish between our ancestors' ideas of God
and close encounters of an extraterrestrial kind?
Paperback: 978-1-78904-852-0 ebook: 978-1-78904-853-7

The Afterlife Unveiled
What the dead are telling us about their world!
Stafford Betty
What happens after we die? Spirits speaking through mediums
know, and they want us to know. This book unveils their
world...
Paperback: 978-1-84694-496-3 ebook: 978-1-84694-926-5

Harvest: The True Story of Alien Abduction
G. L. Davies
G. L. Davies's most-terrifying investigation yet reveals one
woman's terrifying ordeal of alien visitation, nightmarish
visions and a prophecy of destruction on a scale never before
seen in Pembrokeshire's peaceful history.
Paperback: 978-1-78904-385-3 ebook: 978-1-78904-386-0

Wisdom from the Spirit World
Carole J. Obley
What can those in spirit teach us about the enduring bond of
love, the immense power of forgiveness, discovering our life's
purpose and finding peace in a frantic world?
Paperback: 978-1-78904-302-0 ebook: 978-1-78904-303-7

Spirit Release
Sue Allen
A guide to psychic attack, curses, witchcraft, spirit attachment, possession, soul retrieval, haunting, deliverance, exorcism and more, as taught at the College of Psychic Studies.
Paperback: 978-1-84694-033-0 ebook: 978-1-84694-651-6

Advanced Psychic Development
Becky Walsh
Learn how to practise as a professional, contemporary spiritual medium.
Paperback: 978-1-84694-062-0 ebook: 978-1-78099-941-8

Where After
Mariel Forde Clarke
A journey that will compel readers to view life after death in a completely different way.
Paperback: 978-1-78904-617-5 ebook: 978-1-78904-618-2

Poltergeist! A New Investigation into Destructive Haunting
John Fraser
Is the Poltergeist "syndrome" the only type of paranormal phenomena that can really be proven?
Paperback: 978-1-78904-397-6 ebook: 978-1-78904-398-3

A Little Bigfoot: On the Hunt in Sumatra
Pat Spain
Pat Spain lost a layer of skin, pulled leeches off his nether regions, and was violated by an Orangutan for this book.
Paperback: 978-1-78904-605-2 ebook: 978-1-78904-606-9

Astral Projection Made Easy
and overcoming the fear of death
Stephanie June Sorrell
From the popular Made Easy series, *Astral Projection Made Easy* helps to eliminate the fear of death through discussion of life beyond the physical body.
Paperback: 978-1-84694-611-0 ebook: 978-1-78099-225-9

Haunted: Horror of Haverfordwest
G. L. Davies
Blissful beginnings for a young couple turn into a nightmare after purchasing their dream home in Wales in 1989.
Paperback: 978-1-78535-843-2 ebook: 978-1-78535-844-9

Readers of ebooks can buy or view any of these bestsellers by clicking on the live link in the title. Most titles are published in paperback and as an ebook. Paperbacks are available in traditional bookshops. Both print and ebook formats are available online.

Find more titles and sign up to our readers' newsletter at
www.6th-books.com

Join the 6th books Facebook group at
6th Books The world of the Paranormal